W9-AKL-844

The Principal's Guide to the First 100 Days of the School Year

CREATING INSTRUCTIONAL MOMENTUM

Shawn Joseph

EYE ON EDUCATION
6 DEPOT WAYWEST, SUITE 106
LARCHMONT, NY 10538
(914) 833–0551
(914) 833–0761 fax
www.eyeoneducation.com

Library of Congress Cataloging-in-Publication Data

Joseph, Shawn.
The principal's guide to the first 100 days of the school year : creating instructional
momentum / by Shawn Joseph.
    p. cm.
    ISBN 978-1-59667-202-4
1. School principals.   2. Educational leadership.   3. School year—Planning.
I. Title.
    LB2831.9.J67   2012
    371.2'012—dc23

                                                                    2011037092

10 9 8 7 6 5 4 3 2 1

Sponsoring Editor: Robert Sickles
Production Editor: Lauren Beebe
Copyeditor: Laurie Lieb
Designer and Compositor: Dan Kantor, Sierra Graphics, Inc.
Cover Designer: Dave Strauss, 3FoldDesign

Also Available from Eye On Education

What Great Principals Do *Differently*:
Eighteen Things That Matter Most (2nd edition)
Todd Whitaker

Lead On!
Motivational Lessons for School Leaders
Peter Hall

The Fearless School Leader:
Making the Right Decisions
Cynthia McCabe

Communicate and Motivate:
The School Leader's Guide to Effective Communication
Shelly Arneson

Leading School Change:
9 Strategies to Bring Everybody On Board
Todd Whitaker

Creating School Cultures That Embrace Learning:
What Successful Leaders Do
Tony Thacker, John S. Bell, & Franklin P. Schargel

Motivating and Inspiring Teachers:
The Educational Leader's Guide for Building Staff Morale (2nd edition)
Todd Whitaker, Beth Whitaker, & Dale Lumpa

Rigor in Your School:
A Toolkit for Leaders
Ronald Williamson & Barbara R. Blackburn

Problem-Solving Tools and Tips for School Leaders
Cathie E. West

Executive Skills for Busy School Leaders
Christospher Hitch & David C. Coley

The Principalship from A to Z
Ronald Williamson & Barbara R. Blackburn

162 Keys to School Success:
Be the Best, Hire the Best, Train, Inspire, and Retain the Best
Franklin P. Schargel

Supplemental Downloads

Several of the figures discussed and displayed in this book are also available on Eye On Education's website as Adobe Acrobat files. Permission has been granted to purchasers of this book to download these figures and print them.

You can access these downloads by visiting Eye On Education's website: **www.eyeoneducation.com**. From the home page, click on "FREE," then click on "Supplemental Downloads." Alternatively, you can search or browse our website to find this book, then click on "Log in to Access Supplemental Downloads."

Your book-buyer access code is **SLG-7202-4**.

Index of Free Downloads

About the Author

Dr. Shawn Joseph's passion for educating children and adults has led him to serve in a number of positions in the world of education. He has been an English teacher, a reading specialist, a team leader, an assistant principal, a principal, and a central office administrator. He is also the author of numerous peer-reviewed articles focusing on principal preparation, and his research interests include principal preparation, principal development, school improvement planning, and school/community relationships.

Dr. Joseph earned his Bachelor of Science Degree from Lincoln University in Pennsylvania, a Masters in Education from The Johns Hopkins University, and a Doctorate in Education from The George Washington University.

In 2009, Dr. Joseph was honored by his peers as the National Association of Secondary School Administrator's Met-Life Middle School Principal of the Year for the State of Maryland. He was selected as a finalist for the National Principal of the Year Award, but his nomination was withdrawn due to being promoted to become a central office administrator in the school district that employed him. In 2010, Dr. Joseph was the recipient of the American Educational Research Association's Outstanding Dissertation Award in the area of Educational Leadership.

Dr. Joseph is currently the Director of School Performance at Montgomery County Public Schools and an adjunct professor for The George Washington University and McDaniel College. He is married with two children, and he resides in the Washington, D.C. metropolitan area. He can be reached at Shawn@Josephandassociatesllc.com.

Contents

Foreword

Shawn Joseph has created a terrific how-to book for principals. This is not an easy accomplishment. How do you take something as complex as the principalship and present it clearly in a step-by-step guide for others to follow?

I have often benefited from Shawn's ability to take intricate issues, boil them down to their essence, and then build back up with specific strategies and questions. I watched him as a principal dismantle a complex culture and rebuild it piece by piece, never in a rush, but always with urgency and a plan. I saw leaders come from all over the country to see his school and talk to his staff to try to find a little of the "magic." I knew they came for the same reason I had him on speed dial. Those visitors always left with something to do when they returned to their schools; they gained a toolkit of strategies for success. Shawn recreated that kind of magic in this book, which I eagerly recommend to veteran principals, new principals, aspiring principals, and anyone trying to teach or prepare school leaders.

Shawn doesn't try to deal with big theoretical issues, nor does he attempt to cover every facet of the principalship. He provides an essential handbook, focusing on the first hundred days of the school year, and answers the question, "How does a principal build instructional momentum and get off to a strong start to build a culture of teaching and learning?"

The best thing anyone did for me when I became a teacher was give me Harry Wong's *The First Days of School: How to Be an Effective Teacher* (1997). I cherished it. After reading it, I didn't feel overwhelmed by teaching anymore. I immediately had a plan and strategies to implement it. Principals need the same type of support. I wish I had had this book when I was a new principal, when I certainly wasn't thinking of laying foundations, creating systems, or building community. Rather, I was often just concerned with getting the trash out of the cafeteria.

Shawn and I both had the benefit of beginning our careers in a district that prepared us for the principalship. Unfortunately, having district-run principal training programs is not the norm. Routinely, districts scramble to find someone—anyone—to be the principal. After only a year or two of experience, with little or no preparation, good teachers are often thrust into the principalship. This is particularly acute in our urban areas where so many factors exacerbate principal turnover.

According to Shawn, "Finding, retaining, and supporting high-quality principals is still a very difficult task to accomplish." I say that's an understatement. This can seem impossible in many parts of the country. What do you do? How do you help? However, life's experiences have driven Shawn to refuse the status quo. He understands the impact schools have on kids. If you talk to him for just a few minutes, you will see how strongly he feels that every child deserves a good education. He asks, "Why not every kid? Why do some kids get lucky enough to have a good school and others don't?" His research over the last decade has made him realize that the principalship is a critical component to a great school.

Certainly teachers have the most direct influence on a child's learning, but good teachers don't work for bad principals or at schools with high principal turnover. Those schools struggle; no matter how hard an individual teacher might try, he or she can't adequately serve kids in a poor school culture. More than anyone I have ever met, Shawn has committed his energy to the issue of how universities, districts, and communities can ensure that principals are prepared, retained and supported throughout their careers.

Being responsible for leadership development in the seventh largest school district in the country, I ask myself daily, "How do I prepare and support people who have dedicated their lives to such a noble profession?" Principals take on an extremely difficult task—one that has such crucial consequences if they fail. Shawn's message about the need to find, retain, and support principals is the same message that my new superintendent delivered when I arrived in Houston. Dr. Grier, the Superintendent of the Houston Independent School District, told me as soon as I arrived that we had to have a quality principal in every single school. He made it a cornerstone of the district's strategic planning and, despite budget issues, created a leadership development department with an urgent mission to support the district's current and future leaders. His urgency drove me to look for resources and strategies to create a program that supports and develops principals. This is one reason I have Shawn on speed dial and why I eargerly awaited the release of this book.

I am glad to finally be able to provide principals and assistant principals with this resource; I will definitely use it with the administrators I mentor and in the classes I teach. I want to make sure that our administrators are thinking about teaching and learning, not just getting trash out of the cafeteria.

Kevin A. Hobbs
Assistant Superintendent for Leadership Development
Houston Independent School District

Introduction

Imagine you were charged with moving a five-hundred-pound boulder up a very steep hill. Do you think you would be able to do it? This task would be difficult to accomplish for most people, even the strongest of human beings. However, with the proper tools or equipment, such as a crane, you would be able to do it easily. This book is intended to serve as a "tool" to support school leaders, specifically the principal, in accomplishing the very difficult task of building instructional momentum in the first hundred days of school.

The first hundred days of the school year are important, whether you are a new principal or a veteran principal. As a new principal, you will establish basic operating procedures and begin to cultivate the norms of your school. As a veteran principal, you will have the opportunity to reflect on practices from previous years and you can begin the reculturing process as you strive to continuously improve your school for children, parents, and staff. School climates can dramatically change from year to year due to the influx of new students, parents, and staff. As a veteran principal, paying attention to shifts in the dynamic of each constituency and developing organizational structures and processes to proactively guide your school will result in maintaining continued positive momentum as each year passes. As a result, both new principals and veteran principals will find this book, filled with ideas about critical activities to consider in your first hundred days of school, timely and relevant.

The principalship can be a tough, lonely job. Few jobs provide both the level of satisfaction and the level of challenge that the principalship offers. As I reflect upon my first year as the principal of a large, diverse school, sometimes I ask myself, "How did I ever get through that year?" I realize that my success was largely the result of a sustained faith, family support, a patient and passionate staff and community, a strong school district with an effective central support system, and sage advice from veteran colleagues.

I was extremely fortunate. I had all the aforementioned benefits, but the job was still extremely difficult. This reality led me to begin thinking deeply about what it would take to effectively train extraordinary individuals to ultimately become principals who could ensure dramatic results for children's academic achievement. I ended up reflecting on this issue at George Washington University, and it ultimately became the focus of my doctoral dissertation. The same year that I earned my doctorate, I received the 2009 Maryland Association of Secondary School Principals Met/Life Middle Level Principal of the Year Award. The following year, my dissertation was honored by the American Educational Research Association and received the Outstanding Dissertation Award in the area of Learning and Teaching in Educational Leadership–Special Interest Group (LTEL–SIG).

This book originated from my desire to give back to a profession that has given me so much. The research is clear: excellent principals create the conditions necessary for great schools. As a result, I feel a sense of urgency to help principals and aspiring principals create these conditions. Had it not been for veteran colleagues who were willing to share their "best practices" and their resources with me, my experience and my school's experience would have been much different!

As a trained researcher, an adjunct professor, and a practicing administrator who works directly with thirty-four elementary, middle, and high schools, I understand the need for both theoretical guidance and practical advice. Theory is needed to improve practice, but great practices need to be shared to improve school conditions. This book is grounded in practice that has been informed by theory. My intent was to write a book that gives sound, concrete advice, along with useful resources, to school administrators who typically spend sixty to seventy hours per week serving students and families. This book is intended to be a quick read; I know hundreds of administrators who just don't have the time to read extensive discourses as they attempt to balance work with their personal lives. I think it is the duty of "knowledge keepers" and "distributors" of knowledge to share information in a reader-friendly format.

As I suggested earlier, I understand that the principalship is extremely complex, and it was not my intent to make it seem easy in writing this text. In fact, because the principalship is so complex, I have focused the content of this entire book on the instructional aspects of a principal's first hundred days of the school year.

Who Will Benefit from This Book?

My intent was to write this book for school leaders at all levels who are interested in building momentum and laying the foundation for a strong instructional school program. Most veteran administrators and seasoned students of educational administration understand that a principal cannot change the trajectory of student achievement in a hundred days. Most change efforts take at least three to four years to be fully institutionalized in schools. However, in the first hundred days on the job, principals can create momentum that will define how the hard work of improving instruction and raising the achievement of all students will be done. Within the first hundred days, a school community can get a sense of how business will be conducted over the long haul, and instructional staff should understand the instructional priorities and begin to collaboratively define the vision of how administration, school staff, and the community will work together on behalf of children. As such, the first hundred days are some of the most important days of a principal's school year.

School district executive staff members, including superintendents, deputy superintendents, associate superintendents, and assistant superintendents charged with supporting the development of new and veteran principals, will find this text useful. It provides ideas and examples to support reflection and discussion around vision development, instructional leadership, managing politics, data analysis, and strategic planning. Guiding principals through this text, and discussing the feasibility of ideas and concepts, can support new and veteran principals' growth as instructional leaders.

A veteran principal can read this book and gain a fresh perspective on activities, processes, and ideas that can be implemented to reculture a school. The examples provided are level-neutral.

It is my hope that this book gives administrators some wind under their wings to allow them to fly high and strongly during the beginning of the school year. Research has identified the importance of successful transition periods for an executive's overall success (Hill, 2003; Gabarro, 1987; Watkins, 2003). Each chapter ends with a suggested timeline of activities, organized by month, to help leaders identify what they need to consider as they establish themselves and begin the heavy lifting of improving achievement for all students.

For aspiring principals (assistant principals, teacher leaders, central office leaders, and nontraditional future principals), this book offers a conceptual understanding of the complexity of principalship. Such an understanding of the principalship will prepare them to begin the job in the future with confidence and some know-how.

This book will also be useful in a district-level principal training program or a turnaround principal program sponsored by a for-profit or nonprofit organization. Finding, retaining, and supporting high-quality principals is still a very difficult task. School districts and for-profit and nonprofit organizations are thus working to find creative ways to support and retain strong principal candidates (Joseph, 2010). The materials and ideas in this book will support their efforts to foster critical reflection by the program's participants.

This book was also organized with the university professor in mind. The book is not intended to be a primary textbook for a university course. University primary textbooks tend to include more direct references to empirical research. However, I did write it to be a useful secondary text to a traditional university textbook. Graduate schools of education are expected to introduce students to theory in order to stretch their thinking about complex issues. One missing element in many graduate education courses is a solid explanation of practice that puts applicable theories into action. Quite often, in many schools of education across the nation, the practitioner has been forgotten. A rounded graduate school education effectively balances both perspectives. This book should be a useful supplement in an introduction to the principalship course, the internship course, or the instructional leadership/supervision course in a graduate school of education.

Plan of the Book

The rest of this book provides a roadmap to guide school administrators in building the instructional momentum necessary to improve student achievement. This book primarily focuses on ideas to expand leaders' thinking in five key areas, listed below. In many instances, for the purpose of brevity and clarity, detailed descriptions of how to implement some ideas were not included. My future writing will provide much more detail about how to accomplish some of the ideas described in this text for those who would like additional support. Considering these ideas in their totality will provide school leaders with a clear understanding of the scope and thought processes needed to create positive instructional momentum in the first hundred days.

The five chapters of this book address the following concepts:

Vision: Understanding the power of developing a shared vision of excellence and communicating your beliefs to your constituency is critical to your initial success. The power of your school's shared vision will propel you into the future. As the leader of the school, you will need to create the conditions necessary to revisit or to create a shared vision of excellence.

Building your team: Your success as a leader will ultimately depend upon the quality of leaders you choose to keep around you. You'll discover how to assess your initial leadership team and how to effectively work with your colleagues.

Understanding politics: Principals must understand the politics of their positions. This chapter explores the work you'll need to do to build relationships with key constituencies.

Understanding your data: All data tells a story. What is the most critical data for you to understand? How do you build systems and processes to monitor critical data points? This chapter explores the principal's role as the data leader of the building.

Strategic planning: Most schools do not fail because they have poor plans. Schools fail most often due to poor execution of plans. The last chapter suggests a framework for looking at strategic planning and provides timelines of activities to consider as you work to continuously improve student achievement.

These five concepts are not linear, and readers should not think of them as step one, step two, and so on. The chapters can be read sequentially or in a different order based upon your needs. These five concepts are all important for new and experienced principals, but based upon your local context and specific situations, some concepts may be more vital to your success than others.

The book has been organized by the Educational Leadership Policy Standards: ISLLC 2008 (Council of Chief State School Officers, 2008) and National Board Core Propositions for Accomplished Educational Leaders (National Board for Professional Teaching Standards). Reflection questions are included at the end of each chapter to stimulate meaningful conversation about practice. Additionally, each chapter ends with a list of activities and a timeline suggesting when a principal might consider implementing them. The timeline should be modified based upon your local situation. In the back of the book, you will find a Master Timeline for the first one hundred days and a list of suggested additional reading.

Our children deserve quality schools led by quality principals. Our collective collaboration will move us closer to this reality. I hope you enjoy reading this text, and, more importantly, I hope that it helps you to serve children. Feel free to stay connected by contacting me at Shawn@Josephandassoci atesllc.com.

Become the Great Communicator: The Power of a Shared Vision

Activities in this chapter support the following principal leadership standards:

Educational Leadership Policy Standards
➤ **ISLLC 2008 Standard 1:** Education leaders promote the success of every student by facilitating the development, articulation, implementation, and stewardship of a vision of learning that is shared and supported by all stakeholders.
National Board Core Propositions for Accomplished Educational Leaders
➤ Accomplished educational leaders have a clear vision and inspire and engage stakeholders in developing and realizing the mission.

In the year 2009, all across America, the phrase, "Yes, we can" became synonymous with a political movement for change in American politics. Whether you agree or disagree with President Barack Obama's politics, his framing of a message was a masterful lesson that all principals should understand: you need a simple message that can be packaged and communicated to your staff, parents, and students.

People want to know what you are thinking. Let's face it. From the moment you walk into your building as a principal, staff members are stressed! Staff, parents, and students are constantly thinking, "What does the principal want from me? How hard will I be expected to work? How will the principal's actions affect my life?" Your first hundred days of the school year will set the stage not only by answering these questions, but by establishing the processes and systems that you are going to use to communicate your professional beliefs, values, and expectations. More importantly, in the first hundred days, you should collaborate with parents, staff, and students to communicate the school's shared vision of excellence. One major task in your first hundred days will be to determine whether your school has a powerful shared vision already in action or needs to revisit or re-create a shared vision of excellence.

This is a really big, important task to accomplish, but you have no need to worry! The remainder of this chapter will outline some "think-abouts" for you as you work through the processes and systems you will develop to effectively steward a shared vision of excellence within your school community. You'll discover that great oratorical skills are not as important for your success as effective processes and systems of communication.

Your Beliefs and Motivation

You haven't lived in a vacuum all of your life. Your personal experiences have shaped your beliefs, and your beliefs have shaped your leadership style. As the principal, you'll need to reconcile your beliefs with the beliefs that exist in your school. Many leaders fail because they do not take time to understand the system in place. A leader may walk into a building and attempt to impose a new value system on the organization. Bad idea! The system in place was there before you, and it will take a long time to change it. Understanding the culture that exists and starting the conversation about excellence with those aspects that are in line with your beliefs will get you off to a good start.

In an ideal world, your school would share your own beliefs, values, and educational philosophy. In reality, things may be a little different. It is therefore important for you to openly, honestly, and gradually allow the staff, parents, and students to learn what you believe about education and excellence. You are not asking them to accept what you believe, although it would make life easier if they just did what you wanted them to do! What you are doing is saying, "My actions are based upon this set of values that I have lived by, and I want you to understand why I may initially do what I do." This process takes the anxiety and guessing out of your actions. Transitions at the start of a new year are not easy for people, and your constituency needs to know what life is going to be like under your leadership. As the leader of your building, you need to work in a very transparent manner. In addition, you want to openly communicate your beliefs and values in order to give your constituency a chance to connect with you on a personal level. Remember, trust can be built only on a positive, foundational relationship based on common interests, beliefs, and values. Open communication of your beliefs and values can be used to relieve anxiety, create opportunities to connect, and lay a foundation for trusting, positive relationships. It is human nature to search for points of connection with the people that you work closely with in an organization. By modeling the way for your staff and community, you can inspire others to express their values and beliefs openly as they come to understand and accept your leadership.

Over time, you will invite your staff, parents, and students to share their vision of excellence. In this way, you can build or reinforce a community vision that will set the standard for the hard work that lies ahead of you. The following are some suggestions for you to think about as you work to communicate your vision of excellence.

♦ Graphically display your vision of teaching and learning (on a poster, flyers, on the school website, etc.). Share it with staff

Figure 1.1 Personal Core Values and Vision

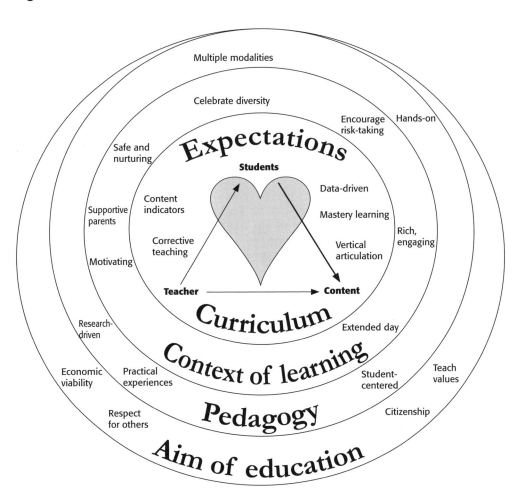

members and parents, and give them an opportunity to talk with you about aspects they agree or disagree with. Collecting these reactions will help you avoid landmines in the future. A sample graphic display is shown in Figure 1.1.

♦ Use your first few community newsletters or the school's Web site to share your educational beliefs and motivations. Include your e-mail address to allow parents, staff, and students to share their comments.

♦ Write a monthly message to parents and display it prominently on your school's website. See Figures 1.2A and 1.2B (pages 6–9).

Figure 1.2A Sample Web Message for Parents (July or August)

I would like to welcome you to Utopia High School. Utopia High School has been in existence since 1994. Our goal is very simple: we want to create a dynamic learning environment where our students can learn and grow.

At Utopia High School, we will show students how much we care for them through our expectations of them. We expect our students to take rigorous courses. We expect them to respect one another. We expect parents to be equal partners in their children's learning. We expect our students to do their best!

We are a large high school, but it is my goal to give families the personal attention you deserve. Our doors are always open for you to come in and visit your child. It is very important for you to know what your child is learning. It is my hope that you will frequently visit schoolnotes.com to keep abreast of your child's classroom assignments.

We are in the process of revising our mission statement and vision statement as a school community. We gathered preliminary feedback from parents, students, and staff this summer. We will continue to gather feedback at the beginning of the school year. Our goal is to clearly articulate our school's belief system and our school vision. A theme for this year is that everything we do will be a matter of PRIDE. I want you and every staff member to be proud of the great things that are happening here at UHS.

During the month of September, we will be having a magazine drive as a school fund-raiser. I'd like to raise money to purchase a mobile computer lab and help fund a Saturday school program to help more UHS students successfully enroll in advanced placement courses. In addition, Back-to-School Night will be on XXXX at 7 p.m. This is an important night when you can meet your child's teachers and learn about your child's "school world."

I hope you find this Web site useful as we continue to improve our ability to communicate with you. I will update this site monthly with upcoming events and reports. I am looking forward to seeing you all on XXXX at Back-to-School Night. If you have any questions in the interim, please give us a call (XXX-XXX-XXXX) or stop by the school. Once again, I am humbled by the opportunity to serve you.

Figure 1.2B Sample Web Message Highlighting Procedural Changes for the Community (September)

We are off and running. We had a wonderful kickoff for the _____ school year. Your children are wonderful, and they have been demonstrating their Utopia Middle School PRIDE by their enthusiasm for learning and their positive behavior.

I'd like to spend a moment addressing some of our new procedures here at Utopia Middle School. These procedures were put in place to help our school maintain a safe, academically rich learning environment.

New Procedures

Common assessments: Each teacher teaching a similar subject will be giving similar weekly assessments. These will allow teachers to discuss instructional practices. The assessments will also allow teachers to regroup students so students who have mastered course objectives can progress, while students who need more time to master course objectives can get the support that they need.

Focus on reading: Each team is in the process of identifying specific content-area reading strategies that will be used in all your child's classes. This process will allow students to "own" a set of reading strategies that will improve comprehension of grade-level and above-grade-level text.

School Notes: You can see what your child is learning and the homework assignments for the week by going to *www.schoolnotes.com*. All you need to do is enter our zip code and find your child's teacher's name.

Morning procedures: Staff members monitoring students are not required to be on duty until 7:25 a.m., so students cannot enter the building until 7:30 a.m. This rule is for their safety. At 7:30 a.m., any student eating breakfast is allowed into the cafeteria. Students must remain there until 7:45.

Between 7:30 a.m. and 7:45 a.m., all sixth-grade students report to the sixth-grade hallway, all seventh-grade students report to the cafeteria, and all eighth-grade students report to the back of the school by the gym entrance. When the weather is bad, eighth-grade students will report to the gym. At 7:45, all students are released from their areas, and they must go to their lockers and report to class by 7:50. Our goal is to minimize wandering through the halls. We expect students to be prepared for learning by 7:55.

Lunch procedures: Students are walked to and from the cafeteria by their teachers. To begin the school year, students in each grade level will sit in alphabetical seating. We follow this procedure for a number of reasons:

- We need to practice emergency lunch procedures.
- Students need to understand proper lunchroom etiquette.
- Adults need to learn students' names (the administrators, counselors, lunch aides, and security team are in the cafeteria).
- Alphabetical seating decreases the anxiety many students feel regarding where they will sit.

When students understand our emergency procedures, demonstrate proper lunchroom etiquette, and seem comfortable following the rules, we will allow students to select their own seats.

We are allowing students to go outside for part of their lunch period to socialize with old friends. If you have concerns regarding this policy, I strongly encourage you to come visit us during a lunch period. You will have a better understanding of what it looks like to monitor 350 high-spirited middle schoolers for thirty minutes a day. ☺

Dress code: Any students wearing clothing that is disruptive to the academic environment will be sent to the office. We will call parents to ask you to bring a change of clothing for your child, or we will offer students a Utopia Middle School shirt. Any student who cannot have a change of clothing brought to school or who refuses to wear a Utopia Middle School shirt will remain in the office for the day.

Student discipline policy: We have streamlined our discipline policy. We expect all students to follow the rules of our school. Here is our school's hierarchy of discipline:

1. Verbal warning
2. Lunch detention/teacher will call home
3. After-school detention/teacher will call home
4. 6 p.m. detention/administrator will call home/parent conference/ student contract
5. Out-of-school suspension/parent conference before student returns to school

Once students are placed on a student contract, they are not allowed to participate in any extracurricular activities except homework help. Once they earn the right to be off the contract, they will be able to participate once again.

I thank you for supporting our schoolwide procedures. Our goal is to ensure your child a safe, orderly, and academically enriching environment. Guaranteeing this for the 1,100 students enrolled at Utopia Middle School is a fun-filled adventure!!

Upcoming Events

Back-to-School Night: Back-to-School Night has expanded from one night to two nights this year. Parents of sixth-grade students are invited to Back-to-School Night on _____, beginning at 7 p.m. On _____ we will have another Back-to-School Night for seventh- and eight-grade parents. Flyers will be sent home during the week of September X, 20XX.

Progress reports: You will be receiving a progress report from each of your child's teachers on _____. This will give you information on how your child is doing in all classes before mid-semester grades are due.

Fall play auditions: On _____, we will begin auditions for the fall play. Encourage your child to participate in this wonderful learning experience!

Contact Information

If you have any concerns, your first point of contact should be your child's guidance counselor. Our counselors are Ms. X (sixth grade), Mr. Y (seventh grade), and Ms. Z (eighth grade). Counselors can be reached at (XXX) XXX-XXXX.

Each grade level also has an administrator. Our grade administrators are Mr. A (sixth grade), Ms. B (seventh grade), and Ms. C (eighth grade). Please feel free to contact your child's grade-level administrator if you cannot reach a counselor or you feel your issue warrants administrative attention.

We all are here to help your child develop into someone special. The world is looking for something special! We continue to be here to serve you. I look forward to meeting you all at one of our Back-to-School Nights. See you soon!

Sincerely,

Principal

♦ Think of a mnemonic device that communicates your educational beliefs and values. At your first staff meeting and your first parent association meeting, share these core values. Allow staff and parents to express their own beliefs and core values.

Figure 1.3A   Sample Summer Letter to Parents

Dear Parents, Guardians, and Students,

We are excited to welcome many of you back and to greet others to our school community for the first time. As the new principal of Utopia Elementary School, I can tell you firsthand that our school's commitment to excellence will not be exceeded by any other school in the country!

Our school's leadership team has worked hard this summer to help us continue the tradition of excellence here at Utopia Elementary School. Our goal is to continually improve our ability to meet the needs of all students and to increase our ability to effectively communicate with parents. Although we have made gains in our students' academic performance over the years, we are not satisfied if any of our students do not meet high standards. We are therefore meeting with parents, students, and staff this summer to identify specific goals in the areas of student achievement, school climate, and parent communication. Our meetings will take place from (date) through (date). I have enclosed an agenda containing the outcomes of the meetings for the week. Please feel free to call the school at (XXX) XXX-XXXX to RSVP if you would like to attend on any day. Over the course of the year, you will be invited to work with us as we monitor our progress in these areas. We will use our parent-association meetings as working meetings to review our progress and gain parent input.

My vision for Utopia Elementary School is for us to constantly demonstrate our commitment to excellence through our expectations for our students. We will show our students how much we care for them by expecting all of them to succeed and excel. The first day of school is (date). School begins at 9:25 a.m. and ends at 4:40 p.m. From the first day of school through the last day of school, you and your children will know, "Excellence is in the air at Utopia Elementary School!"

Sincerely,

Principal

♦ Over the course of the first month of school, host a weekly "meet-and-greet" or "principal's coffee hour." Schedule them at different hours of the day at your school and at local gathering places such as a community center or coffee shop. In these informal settings, share your personal story with the parents of your students. Let them know about your family and your personal journey to the

Figure 1.3B   Sample Summer Letter to Staff

August 2012

Dear Staff,

I am very excited about the start of this school year. It has been humbling for me to see so many staff members here this summer working to make this next year one of the best years in Utopia Middle School's history!

Our school's leadership team has worked hard this summer to help us continue our pursuit of excellence here at Utopia Middle School. Our goal is simple: We want to maximize the potential of *all* of our students. We worked hard to put systematic processes and procedures in place to support students who are not learning.

However, this would not be Utopia School District if we did not have any changes. When you arrive, you will meet ten new full-time or part-time teaching staff members and six nonteaching staff members. You will learn of our new initiatives, and we will continue to build strong relationships with colleagues.

Please come back home at 7:30 a.m. on Monday, August XX, 20XX. You will be greeted with a warm smile and a light breakfast!

Our school's vision statement says that we will collaborate to eliminate the achievement gap, inspire excellence, and teach our students about the value of citizenship. This will be the year that we take one giant step toward this reality. I am looking forward to meeting you all soon.

Sincerely,

Principal

principalship. Discuss your nonnegotiable core values as they relate to educational excellence. Allow the families to share their stories and their personal views as well.

♦ Create a picture show of you, your family, and your professional career. Share them with your staff and parents as an introduction to who you are as a person and an educational leader.

♦ Create a professional school Twitter account, Facebook account, and/or weekly blog so your school community can keep abreast of your life as the principal of the school. These Internet tools can be a powerful communication mechanism allowing you to connect with your school community throughout the year.

♦ Send a welcome letter to parents and staff prior to the first day of school. See Figures 1.3A (page 10) and 1.3B (page 11).

Processes for Gathering Input About Your School Vision

You are going to discover that although your own beliefs and core values are important, they are not as important as your school community's vision of excellence. Vision is one of the most important components of a school community. School leaders who take the power of vision for granted, and who do not spend a considerable amount of time establishing, cultivating, and nurturing a shared vision of excellence, miss an opportunity to inspire greatness from staff, parents, students, and the surrounding community. Most importantly, a leader who does not understand the power of a strong, community-built vision will miss the chance to build trust and a sense of community. A school community's vision should establish the priorities of the school, underlie its organizational structures, and inform the programs and pedagogical philosophies that are encouraged within the school environment.

School staff people will expect you to be able to give their work a sense of direction. As the leader of the school, your job is not to tell them what you want them to do. Your job is to direct them to the vision of the school and ask each stakeholder, "Is our vision compelling enough and focused enough to move our work forward to achieve our definition of 'world-class' status for all our students? What resources, organizational structures, and supports do we need to achieve our vision? How will we communicate our vision so everybody can understand what we are doing and why we are doing it?"

By the time you have reached the status of principal, you've had a pretty successful career. You probably were a model teacher, a strong assistant principal, an intelligent and capable manager in an educational field or in the business world, or a politically astute community leader. Okay, maybe your uncle was the superintendent, but you had to know something about schools! In any case, your understanding of educational issues and how schools work generally exceeds that of the typical parent. My point is that the goals of national and state educational accountability measures may have influenced your philosophies about excellence, but they may not have affected your community's beliefs. I point this out to emphasize that it can be dangerous to be a visionary leader running too far ahead of your constituency. If your community is more concerned with winning the state high-school football championship than with increasing students' performance on the SAT by a certain number of percentage points, that's a tidbit of information that is important for you to know. It will determine the "how to do it" aspect of your work.

Conversely, you may work in an environment where community involvement, defined as parents and the business community actively participating in school-related activities, does not exist. Perhaps parents rarely interact with school personnel except regarding disciplinary actions, and staff members at the school do not see parent or community involvement as an important, integral part of the school's culture.

Typically, whether you serve in a rural, a suburban, or an urban school, there will be a range of parental involvement. Your job as the leader is to assess where your school falls on the continuum of involvement and to energize and engage the community's citizens to actively contribute to their children's academic success. If the parents of your students have not been actively engaged, you will need to work harder to understand the community that you serve and engage its interest. This will be very important work for you because students' success is maximized most effectively when they are supported in all aspects of their lives. A good reference book for you to review on this topic is *Beyond the Bake Sale: The Essential Guide to Family–School Partnerships*, by Henderson, et al. (2007). Even though the work of a school must continue whether the parents and business community actively participate in school activities or not, the vision of the school should not be created and implemented without substantive collaboration with your constituency of parents. As the leader, you will immediately set the tone for the expected level of collaboration within your first hundred days.

Leadership has been defined as the art of mobilizing others to accomplish a task, so you must take the time to understand the level of the parents' involvement before you can adequately inspire them to action. Your community's understanding of educational issues may not be very sophisticated, but that's okay. It's your job to mobilize them and move them forward. As a principal, you recognize that your ultimate responsibility is to increase academic achievement for all students and to ensure that they develop socially and emotionally. You want your students to enter college or the workforce prepared to handle the challenges and complexities of the world. You also want them to be model citizens. The work that you do needs to inspire community members to recognize their role in this process.

Here are some activities that will allow you to inform your parents and community about the state of education at your school and encourage them to begin thinking about what they ultimately want for their children:

Figure 1.4   Survey of Parents' Educational Values

This year at Utopia Elementary School, we will be revisiting our current vision statement. As a part of the process, we would like you to share your personal educational values with us. We will use this information, along with information from our staff and our local business community, to review and, if necessary, revise our vision statement. We appreciate your input in this very important process.

Write a sentence that describes your educational hopes and dreams for your child.
As you think about our school, please list expectations you have for us.
In your opinion, what should our school emphasize to improve students' academic performance?
In your opinion, what should our school emphasize to improve school culture?

Thank you for taking time to provide us with this feedback. In the coming weeks, we will be communicating with you about the process we will use to refine or revise our school vision statement.

♦ Research and share statistics about national high-school and college graduation rates. Compare your school feeder pattern's data with this national data. Be sure to disaggregate by student subgroups. Share the information with your community. Don't be afraid if the results are bad. People need to understand the actual state of the school to rally and move forward if your data does not look good.

♦ Research national earnings data comparing the lifetime earning rates of high school dropouts, high-school graduates, and college graduates. Share the information with your community.

Figure 1.5 Student Survey

Do you speak a language other than English? If so, what?
What language is spoken at home most often?
Are you or your parents from another country? If so, what country?
Are you involved in a sports league outside of school? If so, name it.
Are you involved in other activities outside of school (for example, Boys and Girls Club, karate, dance, Boy Scouts or Girl Scouts, Greek school, etc.). If so, please list them as specifically as possible.
Do you and your family attend religious services outside of your home? If so, identify the name of your place of worship and the town where it is located.

♦ Use PowerPoint to graphically display your student performance data as a way to share your successes and your challenges. Think about how parents and the business community can help you with your challenges, and work to establish a clear structure for them to support the school.

♦ Post pictures of your students throughout the hallways of your building. Have students write under their pictures what they want to do when they grow up; have parents write what they want their children to achieve. Work to ensure that students understand what steps they need to take in order to achieve each dream.

♦ Join your local chamber of commerce to begin building relationships with local business community leaders. Begin educating local business leaders about your school.

Figure 1.6 Student Belief Statement Sheet

Name: _____ Grade: _____

In order to improve Utopia High School, please reflect on your last school year. Think about what you would like to see happen this year to make Utopia High School a better place.

Example:

Issue: Last year, we did not use the computers enough in school.

Belief statement: I believe that all students should have multiple opportunities to use the computer.

Issue:
Belief Statement: I believe that all students should

In the beginning, especially in a school where there has not been active community engagement, you will be working on multiple fronts. You will be working to communicate your beliefs and core values, to understand the core values and beliefs of your community, and to educate your community about the state of education at your school. I have included a suggested timeline of activities at the end of each chapter to help you conceptualize this work clearly, but it is not an exact science. What is most important is that you, as the leader, initiate and encourage a high level of engagement.

Here are some activities to help you understand your community's beliefs and core values:

♦ At your first parent-association meeting and at your first Back-to-School Night, have parents complete a survey about their educational values. Collect the sheets and organize them by topic. At a later parent-association meeting, share the collated lists with the parents. Facilitate a process to establish the community's top five priorities. See Figure 1.4 (page 14) for an example of such a survey.

Figure 1.7 Survey of Staff's Educational Values

This year at Utopia Elementary School, we will be revisiting our current vision statement. As a part of the process, we would like you to share your personal educational values with us. We will use this information, along with information from our parents and our local business community to review, and if necessary, revise our vision statement. We appreciate your input in this very important process.

Write a sentence that describes your educational hopes and dreams for your students.
As you think about our school, please list expectations you have for us as a school community.
In your opinion, what should our school emphasize as it relates to students' academics?
In your opinion, what should our school emphasize as it relates to school culture?

Thank you for taking time to provide us with this feedback. In the coming weeks, we will be communicating with you about the process we will use to refine or revise our school vision statement.

♦ Survey students to identify demographic information and their activities outside of school. This information may help you identify key community organizations that will work with the school to increase student engagement. See Figure 1.5 (page 15) for a sample student survey.

♦ At your first meeting with students, select appropriate grade levels to complete a belief statement sheet (Figure 1.6). Collect these sheets and organize them by topic. At a student assembly, share the collated list with your students. Work with the student government association to narrow the list down to the students' top five priorities.

♦ Collaborate with a nonprofit organization or create a parent outreach team at your school to go into the community at local shopping centers, supermarkets, or neighborhood gathering places to poll community members on what is most important to them as it relates to supporting your school. Collect this information and review it for themes. Narrow the list down to the top five priorities. Your parent outreach team should include a staff member from each grade level and nonteaching staff who are familiar with the community.

♦ At your first meeting with staff, have staff complete a Belief Statement Sheet (Figure 1.7, page 17). Collect the sheets and organize them by topic. At a faculty meeting, share the collated list of parent, student, and staff beliefs. Facilitate a process to reduce your list to the top five priorities for staff.

Packaging Your Vision

Once you have consolidated the staff's, students', and parents' beliefs into a doable, clear list of priorities, the school community will need to identify what your top priorities will be for the next year or two. Equally important, you will need to "package" these beliefs. Packaging is as important as the list itself because proper packaging will enable people to remember your stated beliefs. Author Malcolm Gladwell (2002), in his classic book *The Tipping Point*, describes the packaging process as "the stickiness factor." In essence, this concept answers the questions, "So how do I help everyone understand what I want them to know? How do I help people remember what is important? How can I make our priorities get inside my constituencies' minds, hearts, and souls?" I've found that the use of an acronym is the best way to accomplish this goal in a public school setting. Figure 1.8 is an example of a set of belief statements that have been narrowed down to the top five beliefs and turned into a packaged vision statement.

Figure 1.8 Vision Statement Table

Belief Statement	Simplified Phrase
All students should take responsibility for their own learning.	Personal responsibility
Staff, parents, and students should be respectful to one another.	Respectful interactions
We believe in effort-based intelligence; if students work hard, they should be given opportunities.	Intelligence is effort-based
We celebrate our diversity.	Diversity is celebrated
We want our students to be safe at our schools.	Ensure a safe, positive learning environment

The simplified phrases yield the acronym PRIDE.

There are many other great words that you can use for your acronym. The following is a list of suggestions:

- STARS
- BELIEVE
- INSPIRE
- CELEBRATE
- EXCELLENCE
- ACHIEVE
- EMPOWER
- The 3 Rs or any other letter
- The initials of the school
- VISION
- EXPECT
- NOW
- SUPER
- DOLLAR
- BEST
- GREAT

I'm sure you and your team (or future team) can come up with some other words that may have significance to your school or community. Personalized, short words are even more meaningful when they have local importance. Whatever word you choose, it should be something that all students, even a kindergartner, can remember. Once you have narrowed your vision down to a memorable packaged word, your job is to ensure that your beliefs become a live and vibrant part of your school community.

Systems of Communication to Reinforce the Implementation of Your Vision

Your vision statement should be everywhere you look within your school. The vision statement should be on a banner hung prominently at the entrance of the building. Each hallway should have a banner of your vision statement. Each classroom should have a laminated poster or a large visual display of your vision. I'd even consider creating a mural of your vision statement in the cafeteria and/or gymnasium. The point is that you can't overcommunicate your vision statement, but you can definitely undercommunicate it.

Similarly, your vision statement should be prominently displayed on your school's Web site. The Web site is your welcome card to the world, so be sure to let the world know what you are all about! At the top of newsletters and on your school letterhead, be sure to have your vision statement clearly illustrated.

Think of the many opportunities you have to speak: school assemblies, parent-association meetings, board of education meetings, your morning announcements, and impromptu speeches. There isn't a more powerful way to begin speaking to a group of constituents or your students than sharing your vision statement. Staff, parents, and students always need a reminder of what your school's purpose is; more importantly, everything that your school does will focus on your school vision. As a result, celebrate it and communicate it in every venue in which you represent your school.

Systems to Publicize Your Work

Schools do great work day in and day out. Each day, your staff will touch the lives of children and offer them hope for a better day. Although many students will succeed in spite of their educational opportunities, there are also millions of children who succeed because of the educational opportunities that are offered to them. Conversely, as we look at the news daily, more often than not we see a story about something negative happening in our schools. As the leader of your school, you can do something to change this reality.

Consider establishing a public relations team in your building. Identify one or two key staff members who are great writers and can capture all the wonderful things happening in your school. If you can identify a school photographer, you'll have powerful pictures to go along with your written narratives of events. You should send your local newspaper at least one article per month highlighting something that has happened at your school that is making a difference for your community. The reality is that either you will create an image for your school, or you will allow the media to create an image for you! Consider the following additional suggestions:

♦ Create a quarterly calendar of schoolwide events. Identify someone to write an article for each event and identify a photographer to take pictures. Coordinate a quarterly meeting with your local newspaper's education reporter to review your calendar and schedule possible coverage. If the reporter cannot attend, be sure to send an article and a picture to the newspaper.

♦ Identify your local newspaper contacts and host a breakfast or lunch meeting with them to talk about your school and to open proactive, positive lines of communication with the reporters.

♦ Be sure to highlight a variety of events and activities at your school. Including academic, cultural, and social activities will provide a balanced public image.

♦ If your school district doesn't send your honor roll names to the local newspaper, be sure you do so. This is a powerful way to celebrate the excellence of your students' work, and it sends a message to parents and students that you value high achievement. Post your honor roll students' names on the school Web site and on a prominent hallway display at the school.

♦ Post articles and pictures of events on your school Web site and send articles and pictures to your school system webmasters.

♦ Create a school list-serve and send out daily morning announcements on it. You can also send articles and pictures highlighting activities at your school.

♦ If your school or school system has an automated telephone outreach system, send a weekly, one-minute phone message to parents and students highlighting activities at the school.

♦ Create a PowerPoint display of "pride points" for the school. These are the aspects of the school your staff and parent community should be proud of. This is your opportunity to celebrate milestones compared to previous years. Did you reduce suspensions? Did you increase achievement on local or state measures? Has the number of honor roll students increased? Do you have a wide array of after-school activities? Have staff members or students received local, state, or national honors? What are your school improvement goals? In your PowerPoint display, include pictures of students and staff that represent the full diversity of your school. Post the display on the school Web site. If feasible, place a television in your front hallway and allow this display to roll continuously throughout the day. Update it as your "pride points" grow.

Narrowing your community's beliefs down and ultimately writing a vision statement is tough, collaborative work. This work can easily take three to six months to complete because you should be trying to get as much input from your community as you can. Typically, you can collect a large portion of this information at your Back-to-School Night event if it is well attended. If it is not, think about events you have at your school or in your community that do attract greater participation, such as music concerts, sporting events, and international nights. Don't be in a rush to get this done. It is important to get it done right because your vision statement will guide your work for years to come.

How You Will Live Out Your Vision

As a school, you should revisit your vision, once it is developed, often. As I said earlier, it should be on all of your agendas and at the forefront of your mind. A vision is not worth much if it is only words. Your actions will breathe life into your vision statement.

The work that you do beyond your first hundred days will need to be aligned with the stated goals in your vision statement. Once your vision statement is established, I suggest that you arrange quarterly meetings at which your leadership team and members of your community can look at the programs, activities, and structures at your school to evaluate whether your actions and your vision are aligned. Misalignment will cause confusion and frustration, and you ultimately will not achieve your goals. A powerful vision that parents, students, staff, and the community can believe in and support will give you a strong framework to build future work upon.

Summary

As a principal beginning a new school year, you will have a lot to think about. One of your most important jobs is to inspire a shared vision for your staff, parents, students, and community. It doesn't take lots of charisma to do this. What it takes is thought-out systems and processes. Employ some of the ideas outlined in this chapter and you will be off to a good start. Remember, leaders influence others to do great work. The power of your vision will inspire and influence others to transform your students' lives.

Reflection Questions for Principals

1. What are the beliefs, cultures, and norms that existed in the school prior to your arrival?
2. What are your nonnegotiable beliefs and core values?
3. Whom do you need to meet with to ensure that your Web site, newsletters, hallways, and classrooms display the school's vision statement prominently?
4. What structures have you put in place to review, revise, and communicate the vision statement?
5. How have you aligned the vision statement with your allocation of teacher's staff development time, your financial resources, and your human resources?

Reflection Questions and Activities
for Prospective Administrative Candidates

1. How has your school principal promoted a vision?
2. How has a shared vision of excellence in your school been collaboratively developed?
3. Describe your school community and discuss aspects of your school program that would need to be maintained if your school leadership were to change.
4. Evaluate your school's efforts to communicate the school's vision statement using the following criteria: (a) Is the vision statement prominently displayed on the school Web site? (b) Do newsletters communicate the school's vision effectively? (c) Do school programs align with the vision statement? (d) Have processes been established to periodically review and revise the vision statement?
5. Describe your school's priorities based upon what the school celebrates or how it organizes the instructional staff's time.

Timeline of Activities

July

- ◆ Update the school Web site with a welcome letter and picture.
- ◆ Create a picture show to share with your constituency.
- ◆ Meet with immediate supervisor and/or board members.
- ◆ Schedule meet-and-greets with staff and parents throughout the community.
- ◆ Begin creating a graphic of your beliefs and vision of teaching.
- ◆ Collect belief statements from community and staff.

August

- ◆ Collect belief statements from parents.
- ◆ Identify a public relations team and begin brainstorming activities that will be highlighted.
- ◆ Collect belief statements from the community and staff once more.

September

- ◆ Create a year-long calendar of events and meet with local media.
- ◆ Develop a "pride points" PowerPoint display to share at Back-to-School Night and post on the school Web site.
- ◆ Begin weekly automated calls to parents if available.
- ◆ Begin posting list-serve information, Twitter information, Facebook information, and monthly Web site updates.
- ◆ Collect belief statement surveys from students, community, and staff.
- ◆ Share schoolwide data at Back-to-School Night and at different forums to educate the community about the educational status of the school.

October

- ◆ Begin analyzing belief statements if you have a sufficient number from each constituency group.
- ◆ Begin discussing packaging of the belief statements and developing a draft vision statement to be shared and revised with the community over the next two months.
- ◆ Send honor-roll information to the local newspaper and post throughout the building.

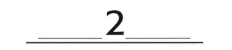

2

Lead Others by Design

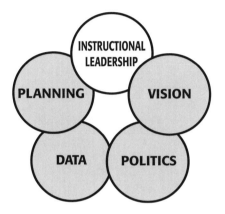

Activities in this chapter support the following principal leadership standards:

Educational Leadership Policy Standards

➢ **ISLLC 2008 Standard 2:** Education leaders promote the success of every student by advocating, nurturing, and sustaining a school culture and instructional program conducive to student learning and staff professional growth.

➢ **ISLLC 2008 Standard 3:** Education leaders promote the success of every student by ensuring management of the organization, operation, and resources for a safe, efficient, and effective learning environment.

National Board Core Propositions for Accomplished Educational Leaders

Accomplished educational leaders:

➢ continuously cultivate their understanding of leadership and the change process to meet high levels of performance

➢ manage and leverage systems and processes to achieve desired results

➢ act with a sense of urgency to foster a cohesive culture of learning

➢ drive, facilitate, and monitor the teaching and learning process

➢ ensure equitable learning opportunities and high expectations for all

---

Hopefully, you now have an understanding of the importance of sharing your beliefs and the power of a shared vision. Another important understanding for you in your first hundred days is to understand the strengths and weaknesses of your leadership team: knowing who is on first and leading them by design.

People will look to you for inspiration. They will want to know that you believe in the vision of your school and that you are working to establish norms to deal with people who do not act in line with the school's vision. The crazy thing is that in your first hundred days, you may not have any idea of the existing vision of your school. To be honest, you may be struggling with your vision of excellence and how it relates to the school. This is not the time to panic, but it is the time for you to do some critical reflection. The reality of leadership is that people expect you to be able to guide them. Your position alone brings about this expectation. John Maxwell (2005), author of *Developing the Leader Within You*, asserts that leadership is influence, nothing more and nothing less, and that the first level of influence is your position. However, I strongly caution you not to let your position go to your head. More importantly, don't think that your position requires you to have all the answers—or any answers, for that matter! If you want to cultivate your ultimate leadership potential, you will need to develop the power of your team.

The reality of the principalship is that the principal cannot be everywhere. As good as I thought I was (all principals have some level of ego or they would not have applied to lead a life-changing organization), I sought to put smarter, more capable people in positions of power around me to move my school. As a principal, you will need people who can effectively communicate and assist you in influencing people within the organization to do what needs to be done. Selecting or keeping the wrong inner circle of leaders within your building will inevitably lead to disaster. This chapter is intended to help you think about your role as the head of a school and ways to assess and monitor the school's leadership team.

Your Role as the Principal of a Building

I remember my first day on the job as a principal. It was July 1, and I can still remember the butterflies that were in my stomach as I walked into "my" building for the first time. I remember my overwhelming feeling of anxiety as the line formed at my door to welcome me into the school. As I smiled and thanked people for taking time to chat with me, the little person inside me was screaming, "Why don't you all just give me a minute to figure out what I just got myself into? I don't even know where the bathroom is in this place!" Once I had a moment of peace, I can remember thinking, "So what am I supposed to do now?"

What is your role? My guess is that it is going to depend upon the culture and priorities of your school district. However, I can tell you what your job is *not*, regardless of school system culture or board of education policies:

- ◆ You are not a secretary. Don't get caught up in reading e-mails and writing memos.

- ◆ You are not a security officer. Don't spend hours conducting investigations.

- ◆ You are not a building services manager. Don't spend hours trying to fix facilities issues.

- You are not a data expert. Don't get caught up in searching for, sorting, and displaying data.

- You are not a business manager or financial secretary. Don't spend hours trying to balance your monthly ledger.

- You are not a subject-area curriculum specialist. Don't spend hours memorizing the outcomes of your state or county curricula.

- You are not the athletic director. Sports are important, but academics are more important.

- You are not a classroom teacher. Don't spend hours designing, planning, and implementing classroom lessons.

- You are not a counselor. Don't spend hours listening and trying to solve everyone's problems.

- You are not a department chair. Don't spend hours trying to communicate departmental expectations to staff members.

- You are not an assistant principal. Your primary job isn't focusing on the nuts and bolts of school operations and discipline.

Ouch! I know that many of you, as you read this list, thought to yourself, "That sounds a bit elitist." My purpose here is not to say that your job is more important than any of the jobs described. Each one of these roles will be extremely important for the success of your school. More importantly, each person who serves in these roles, and any other roles in your school, should be seen as a valued member of your team. As the principal, you will work to support, encourage, and inspire all these individuals so they can perform at high levels to support your students. As the principal, it will be essential for you to understand the knowledge and skills that each of these individuals needs to be successful because you are the primary evaluator in your building. In addition, if you serve in a small school or in a school with limited resources, your job description may in fact assume many aspects of these jobs.

However, you ARE the principal. Your job determines the level of excellence attained in your school. As William Cooke (1995) plainly states in *Strategic Planning for America's Schools*, excellence is narrowly defined. Your job is to develop systems to ensure that all the people described above do their jobs with a high level of fidelity and quality. As the principal, one of the most important jobs you have is as evaluator. You determine whether each individual in your building is meeting the school's standards and is giving 100 percent to ensure that your school is successful. If you get caught up doing the jobs of other people because they aren't doing their job effectively or because you choose to mismanage your time by doing work that could be performed by someone else in your building, you will never function as the leader of a high-performing school. Your job is to make sure people do exemplary work in their job descriptions, so you or other members of your staff do not need to do additional work. Each job description in a school typically carries a full load of responsibilities, and the principal must have the time and ability to objectively monitor and evaluate everything and everyone. Your job entails prioritizing everyone's work and ensuring that staff members clearly understand what they are expected to do and the quality of work they are expected to reach. Again, for the purposes of this text, let's look at your role in monitoring and evaluating your instructional staff.

Assessing Leadership Team Members

Unlike the gift new executives have in the business world, you do not have the power to immediately terminate ineffective leaders or bring in your own team of proven leaders when you become the principal in most unionized school districts. In private schools and charter schools, it may be easier to remove personnel, but many states have due process laws governing the employment of school personnel. There is usually a process that must be followed in order to remove leaders, so when you begin as the principal, you need to understand who you have on your team and if everyone has the capacity to carry out the school's shared vision of excellence. Many new principals rely on advice about their initial team offered by their predecessor, the board of directors, the superintendent, or a central office supervisor. I recommend speaking with these individuals and taking a few notes, but I would never totally trust secondhand information. Here are five suggestions for assessing your leadership team members.

First, read your leadership team members' personnel files. In most districts, as the principal, you will have access to information about your employees. Spend a day in your human resources unit with a list of your school leaders to read their previous evaluations and any other information that has been placed in their files. This will ensure that there are no preexisting major landmines awaiting your arrival. It will also tell you about the quality and type of feedback your new team has received in the past. If the school has an informal file that you have access to, read that as well. This is something you should ask your predecessor about if you have the opportunity to transition. Specifically, ask "Are there any issues that I should be aware of relating to my leadership team's ability to effectively lead at this school? Who are my superstars and why? Who needs support, from your perspective, and why?"

Second, meet with each leadership team member individually. In large schools, this may mean meeting with twenty to thirty people. Although this task is time-consuming, it is very important. You want them to know that you are interested in knowing them and knowing about their abilities. In this initial meeting, I would recommend that you simply ask them to share what they value most about the school and what they think needs to change. Ask about their desire to be a leader in the school. What motivates them to want to be there? What has been their greatest accomplishment at the school or through their leadership in schools? What challenges have they faced? What is their perspective on their department or grade-level team? You should take copious notes during these meetings, and you should fight the temptation to talk. Focus your efforts on listening. You'll have plenty of time to communicate expectations another time. If you talk too much during these first meetings, you may scare people into hiding their true selves. Your goal in this initial meeting is to try to understand the "system in place." You want to know what the values and perceptions of the leadership team were before your arrival.

Third, read samples of each leadership team member's previous observations of teachers. At the elementary level, you may not need to do this: generally, only the principal and the assistant principal conduct formal and informal observations at the elementary level in many states. However, in some secondary schools, teacher leaders may also be a part of the observation process. Depending upon your school district and your contract language, different individuals, including assistant principals, teacher leaders, curriculum leaders, and central office supervisors, may serve as qualified observers in addition to the principal. Based upon who is allowed to write observations in your school, you should spend time reading previous observations from each qualified observer to see the type of feedback observers have historically given to teachers in the school. Reading the reports of qualified observers will tell you a great deal about their communication skills, their ability to communicate instructional priorities and support teachers, and their thinking. You can tell whether people take pride in their work by analyzing their artifacts. Ask yourself, "Does it look like this person took the observation process seriously by providing rich, specific feedback to teachers? Is this person a strong communicator in writing? Did this person complete observations on time? Do all of the observations look similar?" Reading a variety of observations will also allow you to identify consistency with regard to school-wide expectations and instructional priorities across subject areas.

Fourth, have the leadership team members assess how they used their time in the past. The leaders in your building developed their working habits prior to your arrival. Some of those habits are good, and some may be bad. In large buildings where contact with the principal and the administrators may be minimal, your leaders have done what they have valued or what your predecessor valued. You want to know what they have done, so you'll know how to assist them with the change process if you need to change the way things are done. One useful activity is to ask your leadership team members and your administrators to complete a pie chart identifying the percentage of time they engage in the following activities per week: (1) formally and informally observing teachers if it is appropriate, (2) planning for department or grade-level meetings, (3) managing budget items, (4) leading cohorts of teachers in planning, (5) planning staff development activities, (6) monitoring data such as students' grades and unit assessment data, and (7) other activities. This pie chart will be most meaningful for you if you use the criteria that the leadership team members are evaluated upon as your areas for them to quantify. This information can be a powerful tool for you as you communicate your expectations for how you would like your leaders to utilize their time. Their feedback will reveal their perceptions of how they use their time and, more importantly, allow you to engage in meaningful dialogue about what is important. You will also be able to develop strategies to eliminate barriers to achieving your priorities. The key here is that you are digging deeper into understanding the system that has been in place prior to your arrival.

Finally, review your school district's evaluation criteria for each leadership team member's job description if one exists, and narrow the focus down to three or four measurable priorities. Many districts have spent a considerable amount of time and research identifying evaluation standards for administrators and school leaders. Conversely, some school districts, private school networks, and charter schools have not established clearly written job descriptions for leadership team members. Other schools have antiquated job descriptions that are no longer appropriate. Hundreds of different evaluation criteria are used across the country, and the complexity of these evaluation criteria varies from district to district.

Regardless of the criteria that are used in your school district or school, most school employees appreciate clearly understanding what the principal's priorities are. Very few people can do everything exceptionally well! When I was a principal, I understood that I probably would not find perfect people—people who were exemplary in each of the numerous standards they would be evaluated upon—but I did expect people to be exemplary in a few areas. I had different standards for different departments because I was evaluated on certain criteria that were connected to certain departments. To clear up any ambiguity and to eliminate the common saying, "No one can do all the things we are expected to do," I recommend that as the principal, you meet with each of your leadership team members to give them in writing your three or four priorities for the year. Be clear that based upon the priorities for the school, you are going to place an emphasis on the list of three or four criteria that you present. Be explicit about your vision of what you expect to see accomplished. Give your leaders clear, measurable goals that they will be responsible for achieving. Most importantly, develop a schedule of checkpoints throughout the school year when they will show how they are working toward achieving the goals that have been set for them. These are times when you can give your leaders direct feedback on their work and make adjustments to your original plan. For some of your leaders, this will be an easy process because they will be fully prepared with the skills, knowledge, and dispositions that you have communicated. Others will need specific training to be able to achieve what you would like them to do. It is important for your leaders to openly reflect upon their ability to do what you are asking, and it will be more important for you to clearly put in writing job-related support that you will give your leaders to achieve these goals. If you do not create a professional development plan with your leaders to support their success in executing priorities, the perception may be that you are intentionally setting your leaders up for failure. This can negatively affect school culture and your ability to lead the entire group. Conversely, when people are supported to achieve a small number of clear, focused, measurable goals, they will improve and execute, or they will realize that the job is too much for them and can be at peace stepping down from the position. It is rare for someone to receive support, receive clear feedback, underperform, and still want to keep the job. Problems occur when people (1) do not know how they are doing, (2) think they are doing a good job, (3) are unclear about what they are expected to do, or (4) feel as though they have not been supported adequately in achieving stated goals.

Your school's success depends upon the quality of the leaders who surround you. Do not make assumptions about the quality of your leaders or their ability to do the job. As the principal, you have the power to make everything very clear so leaders can be successful. See Figure 2.1 (page 34) for a sample of a team or department action planning template and Figure 2.2 (page 36) for a sample professional development plan.

Figures 2.3A and 2.3B (pages 38 and 39) provide sample letters that the principal can send to a secondary department chairperson and an elementary reading specialist to express the expectations for the coming year.

Figure 2.1 Sample Department or Grade-Level Action Plan

Name: _____   Department or Grade Level: _____

Department/Grade-Level Action Monitoring Plan

1. **Identify the focus of your department/grade level's school improvement efforts this year.**

2. **State #1 as an outcome. (By the end of _____ I will _____ so that _____.)**

   By the end of the year, teachers in the science department will have increased their ability to differentiate processes and resource materials so that student performance will improve.

3. **How will you and others know that you have achieved your outcome? What evidence or data will you have to verify that you have attained your outcome? (Ongoing evidence is shared at monthly meetings with administrators.)**

   Throughout the year, I will share the following evidence of attainment:

   ◆ Samples of student work will be analyzed and discussed with science teachers.

   ◆ Grades will be monitored monthly and discussed with science teachers.

   ◆ Formal and informal observations will be conducted of all science teachers. Science teachers will receive at least two formal observations. Science teachers in their evaluation year will receive four formal observations.

   ◆ Agendas of science teacher meetings will be maintained and notes regarding next steps will be maintained.

   ◆ Staff development will be provided and we will discuss success and challenges as a group. Notes will be maintained.

   ACTION PLAN: In the space below, identify the actions you will take to achieve your outcome, the ongoing evidence you will present at school improvement meetings, and your anticipated timeline for actions.

Action	Evidence	Timeline	Date of Completion

Figure 2.2 Sample Middle School Expectations for Administrators, Department Chairs, and Team Leaders

---

Objectives

♦ Identify administrative support structure for the school year.

♦ Clarify roles of team leaders and department chairperson.

♦ Prioritize roles of team leaders and department chairperson.

♦ Identify barriers to achieving the priorities.

Administrator Support by Department

♦ (Name) will evaluate the Math Department.

♦ (Name) will evaluate the Math Department Chairperson and the Staff Development Teacher.

♦ (Name) will evaluate all administrators.

♦ (Name) will evaluate the ESOL/Foreign Language Department, Special Education Department, and the Alternative I program.

♦ (Name) will work with the 7th grade team and evaluate 7th grade team leaders.

♦ (Name) will evaluate the English/Reading Department, PE/Health Department, and Computer Applications.

♦ (Name) will evaluate the English Department Chairperson, the PE/Health Department Chairperson, and the 8th grade team leaders.

♦ (Name) will evaluate the Science, World Studies, Music, and Art Departments.

♦ (Name) will evaluate the Science Department Chairperson, World Studies Department Chairperson, and the 6th grade team leaders.

Structure Change

♦ All administrators will give the principal a monthly update on their departments.

♦ All administrators are expected to have a formal meeting with their department chairperson two times per month.

♦ A written action plan will be created for each department chairperson and his or her department.

♦ Feedback will be given in writing.

Structure Expectations

- Each administrator will continue to meet with his or her grade level team leaders weekly.

- The principal will connect with team leaders formally monthly during one of the pre-set meetings with the grade level administrator.

Communication Between Department Chairperson and Team Leaders

- If there is a teacher on a grade level team who needs support, the team leader should share his or her concern with the grade level administrator.

- The grade level administrator will address the concern at an administrative meeting.

- The administrator for the content area will set up a meeting with the department chairperson and team leader to develop a written plan of support.

Prioritized Expectations for Department Chairpersons

- Develop a walkthrough schedule for your department. You should visit teachers weekly. A walkthrough schedule template will be developed.

- A written informal observation form should be given to the teacher and the content area administrator.

- Write formal observations. Send them to the content administrator and cc the principal.

- Develop protocols for staff within your departments to look at student work.

- Develop protocols for staff within your departments to look at data.

- Monitor the grade books of department members.

Prioritized Expectations for Team Leaders

- Create a professional, collaborative environment on your teams.

- Establish clear kid talk procedures that focus on our targeted students. A clear process should be defined.

- Establish clear structures for teams to work collaboratively.

- Lead the collaborative effort to celebrate student achievements and plan field trips.

- Monitor team absenteeism.

Figure 2.3A Sample Expectations Letter for the English Department Chairperson

To: Jane Doe, English Department Chairperson
From: Shawn Joseph, Principal
Subject: Prioritized Responsibilities for the 2011–2012 School Year
Date: August 27, 2011

The purpose of this memorandum is to summarize a conversation we had on Friday, August 26, 2011, regarding your prioritized duties and responsibilities as the English Department Chairperson at Utopia High School.

In the meeting, we discussed our school's vision, which states that we will eliminate the achievement gap and ensure that all students are college and career ready. To accomplish this goal, we will need to focus our efforts to improve teaching and learning. As such, the following were identified as your top priorities as the English Department Chairperson:

- Conduct formal and informal observations of teachers within your department weekly. A schedule will be created, and you will provide the administrator supervising the English department formal and informal observation data every two weeks.
- Provide appropriate staff development to English department members based upon students needs, monthly at a minimum, to support English teacher's growth. Facilitate the process of identifying outside resources that are needed to support English teachers' growth.
- Maintain a portfolio of students' work by grade level from members of your department. Student work should be discussed with department members monthly, and the portfolio of work will be reviewed by the administrator working with your department.
- Monitor English teachers' grade books monthly. You should review each department members' grade book with them to ensure that an appropriate number of assignments are administered and to ensure that grades are evaluating curricular outcomes. Department grade distributions should be analyzed quarterly by student subgroups.
- Facilitate grade level data meetings with English teachers analyzing students' work, identifying instructional areas of strength and weakness, and planning next steps to support students.

These five areas are critical to our school's success. As discussed, we will schedule quarterly meetings to discuss your progress as it relates to these five areas. I am looking forward to supporting you this school year as we achieve the goals of our vision statement.

Figure 2.3B Sample Expectations Letter for the Reading Specialist

To: John Doe, Reading Specialist
From: Shawn Joseph, Principal
Subject: Prioritized Responsibilities
Date: August 29, 2011

The purpose of this memorandum is to summarize a conversation we had on Friday, August 26, 2011, regarding your prioritized duties and responsibilities as the Reading Specialist at Utopia Elementary School.

In the meeting, we discussed our school's vision, which will prepare students to excel in the globally competitive world. To accomplish this goal, we will need to focus our efforts to improve teaching and learning. As such, the following were identified as your top priorities as the Reading Specialist:

♦ Monitor and support teachers in the development of collaboratively created Reading formative assessments in grades K–5. Maintain a portfolio of these assessments to be discussed with the principal.

♦ Facilitate reading data action meetings in grades K–5 that review formative assessment data with teachers. Based on formative assessment data, facilitate instructional planning meetings with teachers to ensure students are appropriately retaught and reassessed as needed.

♦ Provide appropriate reading staff development to K–5 teachers based upon students' needs on a monthly basis during faculty meetings and collaborative planning meetings.

♦ Monitor the performance of students in Reading, and recommend appropriate reading intervention programs before school, during school, and after school for students that need additional support.

♦ Collaborate with the leadership team to develop grade level reading observation templates to support the supervision of reading instruction.

These five areas are critical to our school's success. As discussed, we will schedule quarterly meetings to discuss your progress as it relates to these five areas. I am looking forward to supporting you this school year as we achieve the goals of our vision statement.

Who Needs to Fill Time on Your Calendar?

As the principal of your school, it is essential that you develop structures and establish schedules to effectively influence key individuals in your building who are charged with getting results by improving students' lives. The larger the building is, the more difficult it is to influence the culture of the school. One of the first major jobs you will need to accomplish as a principal is to identify those key people you need to meet with frequently. Everybody is going to want to meet with you, but you cannot allow other people to control your calendar. Good leaders do not wait for their calendars to be filled up by people wanting to discuss their own issues. Good leaders fill other people's calendars with topics the leader would like to discuss.

In this era of accountability, leaders are measured by their ability to impact students' performance data. Different states and local school districts have different accountability measures, but all states and districts have something. As the principal, you should schedule a block of time to meet with each leadership team member who directly impacts student performance data that you will be held accountable for improving. These meetings may not seem urgent, but they are extremely important for the long-term success of the school and the principal.

For example, if a state administers tests in reading and mathematics every school year, school performance will be expected to improve annually within a number of student subgroups. The principal of a middle school in this environment should schedule meetings at least twice a month with the math department leader, the English department leader, and any other leaders who work with teachers of math and English or reading. An assistant principal may be in charge of observing and evaluating one of these departments. In that case, the assistant principal would either be present at these meetings or meet with the principal frequently to provide updates and share artifacts regarding progress toward the attainment of outcomes for the department being supervised. Principal leadership is about instructional leadership. Instructional leadership can be defined as the principal's ability to improve the quality of instruction and the quality of student learning by working through others in a school to achieve dramatic results. More simply defined, instructional leadership is the leader's ability to inspire impact within the classroom through others. There are times when an assistant principal will have more instructional know-how than the principal in a particular content area. In those instances, it is not a bad idea to allow the assistant principal to take the lead with a team of teachers. However, the principal should work with the assistant principal to learn how to achieve increased results and should also be present at meetings to verify that the work is getting accomplished effectively and to provide feedback to the assistant principal.

A trap that principals fall into is that they "trust" too easily so as to not look like a micromanager. Part of a leader's job is to search for evidence of achieving results, and this can be done without decreasing morale or taking power away from individuals. The next section of this chapter will describe what the process of frequent meetings with key leaders might look like in a school.

Structured Meetings with Instructional Leaders

It always drove me crazy to sit through an unproductive meeting. Time is the enemy when you are interested in getting results for students, so principals need to make sure that meeting time is used productively within the schoolhouse. We expect good classroom instruction to begin with clear outcomes, and principals should expect their meetings to be the same way. Similarly, meetings should end with a summary of what was discussed, listing clear action steps, persons responsible, and deadlines for the completion of the work. Without this type of accountability, it is very easy to fall into "talking about doing something mode" as opposed to "doing something mode." Figure 2.4 (page 42) is a template that can help you organize your meetings.

Meetings with your key leadership people should always be focused on students' outcomes. Therefore, ask leadership members to bring artifacts that illustrate their supervision and monitoring of student achievement. Artifacts should include their formal and informal observations of teachers, an analysis of students' grade data and ongoing assessment data, drafts of meeting agendas and training materials from agendas, and samples of students' work. Monitoring these key artifacts will allow you to assess the degree to which schoolwide initiatives have been successfully implemented, and it will also give you critical one-on-one time with your leaders to assess their ability to lead and monitor student performance. The following are some ongoing questions that should be asked at such meetings:

♦ What is the quality of feedback teachers are receiving about their instruction and its effect on students' learning?

♦ Are there systems in place to monitor group analysis of student data and individual analysis of student work?

♦ Is there evidence that leadership members and teachers are looking at student work and analyzing data?

Figure 2.4 Meeting Organizer

DESIRED OUTCOMES

Time	Agenda Item	Facilitator

ACTION ITEMS

What?	Who?	By When?

♦ Are next steps, based upon students' needs, clearly identified for teachers?

♦ Is the feedback cycle for teachers seamless?

Your job is to develop systems that affect student outcomes within your building. These questions are the foundation for systems to ensure that work is aligned and focused on student achievement. Let's look at each one of these questions in more detail.

Quality Feedback for Teachers

It has been my experience that in schools that are not thriving and where the quality of instruction is not strong, there is a limited amount of meaningful feedback systemically given to teachers. The principal and the leadership team in these schools are not a presence in the classrooms. The quality of instruction in a school is largely dependent upon the quality of feedback that teachers receive. As principal, one of your most important jobs will be to ensure that each teacher receives timely, quality feedback.

So what does quality feedback look like? Lots of researchers and practitioners have contributed to this discussion over the course of the years. I subscribe to the idea that feedback should be based upon evidence of student learning, not focused on teacher behaviors. There are lots of great performers with effective stage presence in American public schools. On the surface, it looks like these teachers are doing a fantastic job. However, according to their student performance data, large numbers of their students continue to fail. Stage presence and knowing how to communicate in an engaging way are definitely important. However, at the end of the day, are students in the classroom learning? If not, then feedback should be directed toward the teacher to investigate what can be done to improve student performance. Observers should still commend and reinforce good habits such as having mastery objectives, presenting information in a clear format, providing appropriate wait time, randomly calling on students, and summarizing lessons. Books like Saphier's (2008) *The Skillful Teacher* clearly and artfully describe good teaching practices. As a provider of feedback, you should be explicit about determining whether students learned concepts. If not, you should foster reflection so teachers can understand the causes. The only way to do this is to begin discussions with an analysis of student work.

Observation formats vary from district to district. Some observation tools are checklists of criteria that are expected to be met in the classroom. Other observation tools are narrative discussions in which the observer makes claims about teaching that are supported with evidence. Figure 2.5 (page 44) and Figure 2.6 (page 46) show sample preobservation and postobservation forms. Regardless of the observation and evaluation format that is used in a district, almost all school districts require a postobservation conference between the observer and the observed teacher to reflect upon the lesson and the teacher's practices. As shown in the sample postobservation conference write-up in Figure 2.7 (page 47), a postobservation conference should provide a rich discussion of the teacher's work based upon school priorities; provide evidence that the observer looked at student work as part of the discussion; and spark reflection and provide teachers with explicit next steps for their continuous improvement.

Figure 2.5 Preobservation Form

Teacher: Date & Time of Observation:

Grade: Period:

What is the intended mastery objective for the lesson?
How many students from each NCLB (No Child Left Behind) subgroup are present in your class?
What are your teaching objectives for this particular lesson?
Was there a preassessment for this unit of study? How do you plan to evaluate student achievement of these objectives?
What materials will you be using to support this lesson (textbook, novel, handouts, etc.)? Will differentiation be incorporated into this particular lesson? If so, how?

Please check items on which you would like specific feedback:
- ❑ Questioning techniques and wait time
- ❑ Checking for understanding
- ❑ Use of instructional aids
- ❑ Classroom routines and procedures
- ❑ Motivational techniques
- ❑ Classroom management techniques
- ❑ Teacher's delivery and clarity of delivery
- ❑ Pacing of the lesson and momentum shifts
- ❑ Student participation
- ❑ Differentiation strategies incorporated into this lesson

- ❏ Evidence of effective planning and provisioning
- ❏ Use of multiple assessments (formal and informal)
- ❏ Use of bulletin boards, portfolios, and display of student work
- ❏ Key messages
- ❏ Literacy strategies
- ❏ Culturally relevant teaching
- ❏ Rigor
- ❏ Engagement

List anything you would like me to know about this class as a whole.

Looking at Student Work

The most important data schools have at their disposal are students' work. Many schools spend countless hours collecting and displaying unit assessment data, reading and math assessment data, and data that show how much students have learned at a point in time. These data sources allow administrators to quickly locate areas of strength and weakness within a building or a school district, but I do not think this information is meaningful to teachers in any real way. The problem is that this type of data takes time to be computed, organized, and distributed to teachers, and as a result, teachers do not use this information to reteach or reassess. It is more effective to find a way to frequently analyze students' work in order to make instructional decisions based upon the findings. As the principal of your school, it is your job to organize your teachers' work in such a way that this is an expectation that is monitored. We'll discuss this process in more detail in Chapter 4.

Clearly Identifying Next Steps for Teachers

I mentioned the importance of feedback for teachers as it relates to the quality of instruction earlier in this chapter. Feedback, whether it affirms what a teacher is doing well or identifies areas of growth, is vital. As a principal, you need to ensure that teachers get proper feedback from individuals who are responsible for observing and evaluating your instructional program. I have seen many observation reports that affirm teachers' behaviors without critically discussing how to support teachers' growth. As a principal, you should constantly be thinking about ways to coach faculty members to improve their teaching, as evidenced by improved student outcomes. Within your first hundred days, devote some time to understanding the quality of

Figure 2.6 Sample Postobservation Conference Protocol

What was the mastery objective for the lesson?
Did students meet the objective by the end of class?
How do you plan on assessing the objective?
Share some examples of students' work that show students' proficiency on assignments. In addition, share examples of students' work that show students' failure to meet the standard on assignments. What are your next steps?
What were some management strategies you used effectively in the lesson?
What were some instructional strategies you used effectively in the lesson?
How are your African American and Hispanic students performing? What have you done to improve their achievement? Explain.
What literacy strategies are you working on to help your below-grade-level readers? Have they been effective? Explain.
What would you do differently if you were to redo this lesson?

Figure 2.7 Sample Postobservation Conference Write-Up

In the postobservation conference, participants discussed the lesson and reviewed student work.

Utopia School District Criteria I: Teachers are committed to equity and excellence.

The observer said that if he had not known beforehand this was a special education class, he would not have been able to tell that it was a class of students with special needs. Teacher B responded, "My students deserve to be challenged. I'm going to do everything I can do to ensure that they learn at high levels. My students can think at very high levels. They just need me to accommodate for them so that they can adequately show what they know."

Utopia School District Criteria II: Teachers demonstrate pedagogical knowledge within their subject area.

We discussed the instructional accommodations her students need to be successful. Teacher B indicated that most of her students have a scribe accommodation (11 out of 12 students). This has been a challenge, but she has worked to make sure that all students' needs are being met. She indicated that most of her students read at the first- or second-grade level, and they have a read-aloud accommodation (7 out of 12 students). She said, "As a result, once I go over the initial mini-lesson, the teacher's aide and I place the students into small groups. I use the technology hub with the five computers in my classroom daily because I do have students who are motivated to write using the computers. The teacher's aide and I can then scribe for the other students without breaking the flow of instruction. I work closely with the reading specialist to identify reading materials that students can read at their level for practice, but I'll bring students together and I will read text at their grade level because their hearing capacity is much stronger than their independent reading levels."

The observer asked Teacher B to share an example of student work and an example of how she had been accommodating for students. Teacher B gave the observer a paragraph that students wrote after they read the short story "Harrison Bergeron." Students' written work indicated that students are not strong writers. There were errors in spelling, grammatical use, and clarity. This reaffirmed the need for Teacher B to model writing for her students and to provide the students with structure for their writing. In the paragraph that was analyzed, Teacher B accommodated students by giving them a topic sentence and a closing sentence. She said, "I've found that modeling for my students has really improved their writing. Students know that all their written work should be revised if it does not meet the standards that have been set by the model. Once I review students' writing using our standard writing rubric, students must rewrite their work to meet the standard. I have seen tremendous growth in students' understanding of the writing process. However, as you can see, we still have lots of work to do helping students understand the rules of grammar and how to write more concisely. Many of my students have severe language-based disabilities. Spelling is difficult for them, but they are much better when they use a computer as an accommodation. I encourage them to practice their spelling, and we have mini-lessons to support their spelling growth prior to their using the spell-checker on the computer."

Teacher B also shared a vocabulary quiz students completed based on Orwell's *Animal Farm*. The quiz was accommodated by giving the students a word bank.

We discussed the literacy strategies that Teacher B is using with her students. She has begun to systematically incorporate reciprocal teaching into her classroom activities.

Teacher B said that she has not utilized many short stories this school year. The "Harrison Bergeron" short story was the first one used this year. Teacher B said, "The curriculum is new to me, so I don't even know where to go to find good short stories, to be honest. My students enjoyed this short story, but it was very difficult for them." The observer noted that by reading short stories, students can be exposed to a larger variety of materials at different levels. Students will also be exposed to a larger variety of background information and can analyze different literary structures more effectively. Teacher B stated, "That makes sense. I will contact the reading specialist and the English department lead teacher to identify some appropriate short stories to consider. Using short stories can support me as I work on utilizing the reciprocal teaching strategy as well because there is a quick beginning, middle, and end in short stories."

Utopia School District Criteria III: Teachers analyze and monitor student performance data.

An analysis of Teacher B's grades as of 10-20-XX indicated six As, four Bs, and two Cs in this class. There were four graded assignments, including two homework assignments and two graded assessments. The observer said that this is not enough graded feedback for students. Students should receive at least two opportunities for graded feedback weekly, and rubrics should be used with written assignments. All of Teacher B's students are Hispanic or African American, and all are targeted for additional support in order to gain proficiency for the state assessment. Teacher B agreed, "You are right. I do need to assess more. I've been a bit overwhelmed learning the new curriculum and I've been learning my students' interests and needs. Quarter one has just ended. I'll make a conscientious effort to grade more consistently during quarter two."

In regard to her students' grades, Teacher B said, "I do accommodate for students, and their grades reflect those accommodations. Students are working hard and are achieving, but it is due to the modifications that have been made. I am working with my special education lead teacher to better understand how to grade my students. I don't want parents to think that the A means they are achieving on grade level when their work has been accommodated, but I do want to validate the progress that I see."

The observer agreed that this is a discussion that needs to be shared with the entire special education department. As Teacher B noted, grades should communicate to parents how students are performing on grade-level indicators and expectations. If they do not, it should be communicated to parents of special-education students at the meeting that modifications have been made, and those modifications should be shared with parents in writing.

Follow-Up

Based upon this observation, Teacher B should do the following:

♦ Meet with the reading specialist to discuss the reading needs of her class. She should identify a list of appropriate short stories for her students to read. This meeting should be held by November 15.

♦ Meet with the special education teacher leader to discuss grading practices. The special education teacher leader should also share best practices for managing assessment practices on a weekly basis. This meeting should be held by November 15.

Summary

Teacher B is in her first year as a special education teacher at Utopia Middle School. She demonstrates a passion for equity, and she is working to learn the Utopia School District curriculum for eighth-grade English. Teacher B modifies students' assignments to teach them at their instructional level, but she also challenges students to master grade-level materials with appropriate accommodations. She utilizes technology and her teaching aide to support her in meeting students' needs. Teacher B's next observation should focus on her progress in identifying and utilizing appropriate short stories for her students. The observer should also seek evidence of reading progress as Teacher B continues to utilize the reciprocal teaching strategy. Finally, the next observation will investigate Teacher B's progress with providing students more timely feedback as evidenced in her grades. As a first-year teacher, Teacher B is adequately progressing at this time.

feedback that historically has been given to the teachers in your building by reading the previous year's observations and evaluations. In your review of these documents, pay particular attention to the focus of the observer's written feedback. Did the observer's observations reflect an ability to offer teachers next steps or areas of focus that were based upon their students' achievement data? Were the teachers challenged to learn how to do something more effectively, and encouraged with supports and timelines? Were exemplary teachers encouraged to serve as mentors or classroom models for other teachers?

Teachers should be "stretched by design" and exemplary teachers should be utilized to replicate their excellence. The most important, but often neglected, element of the teacher observation process is the follow-up actions stemming from the postobservation conference. School leaders who want to systemically ensure dramatic results in their schools will spend a great deal of time making sure that an opportunity to stretch teachers by design is not missed.

Feedback Should Be Seamless

As the principal of your school, you are in charge of ensuring that there are systems to provide teachers with quality feedback. Thinking through these systems and refining them is essential because, after all, your work is about improving student achievement. Teachers are the vehicle through which this goal occurs.

Unfortunately, many teachers do not adequately develop their skills because the feedback that they receive is isolated, fragmented, confusing, or overwhelming. To illustrate this point, let me describe a scenario that is common in many schools across America.

Cindy is a first-year high-school English teacher. In her school district, the English department leader, the assistant principal, and the central office English supervisor are all considered qualified observers. Any of these individuals can observe Cindy, and their feedback can be used as part of her evaluation. The teachers' contract in Cindy's school district requires that a minimum of three formal observations during the course of the school year should be included in a teacher's evaluation. As a practice at Cindy's school, the principal has decided that all teachers that are in their evaluation year will receive four observations, with new teachers potentially receiving additional observations as needed. At the beginning of the school year, the principal creates an observation schedule to ensure that Cindy is appropriately observed. The English department leader will observe Cindy during the third week of school. The assistant principal will observe Cindy at the end of November. The central office English supervisor will observe Cindy in January. Finally, the assistant principal will observe Cindy again in March. If additional formal observations are needed, the principal will observe Cindy in May.

In secondary schools across the country, this distribution of responsibilities is typical. Large schools need to rely upon multiple people to support the observation and evaluation process. The challenge is that if this process is not coordinated, Cindy may receive feedback that fails to help her build her skills systematically because she is being pulled in many different directions by many different observers.

For example, the English department leader's observation of Cindy in September recommends that Cindy should work to establish a clear behavior management process in her classroom to manage students' poor behavior. In November, the assistant principal recommends that Cindy should focus on asking her students questions demanding higher-order thinking. In January, the central office English supervisor recommends that Cindy should focus on making her classroom more student-centered and increasing her students' collaborative learning opportunities. When the assistant principal returns in March, he is concerned that he does not see clear evidence of higher-order thinking strategies, and he does not understand why the class is so chaotic while students work in groups.

As you think about one of the most important jobs you will have as a principal, providing teachers with meaningful feedback, you should consider how to coordinate the process so teachers will receive feedback that allows them to build their skills without pulling them in multiple directions. Consider the following questions:

- ♦ How will I get feedback from the leadership team and staff about what our instructional "look-for" priorities will be in observations?

- ♦ How will I monitor whether observations are completed in a timely fashion by qualified observers?

- ♦ How can I ensure that all my qualified observers are communicating with each another so each observation builds upon the recommendations from the previous observation?

Your ability to think through your processes to answer these questions will put you ahead of the curve in your first hundred days of school!

How You Will Inspire and Motivate Your Leaders

This chapter deals with your ability as a principal to lead by design. I've discussed the necessity of thinking about your organizational structures and how you use time. I've asked you to consider assessing the players on your team and what their work will look like as they execute. As a leader, you can do all these things well and still have tremendous difficulties if you forget one key aspect of leadership: inspiration.

People need to feel a sense of purpose in the work they do. Serving as a school employee has never been easy. In this era of accountability, most jobs in the schoolhouse can be described as stressful. Your job as principal has the influence to create the conditions in which people work. What you value, monitor, and communicate will frame the culture of your school. If a school has a culture problem, attention should be paid to the person leading that school: the principal. Conversely, you can develop systems that keep people motivated and bring the best out of each employee. The measure of great leaders is their ability to bring out the best in other people.

As stated earlier, how you structure people's work in the schoolhouse has the capacity to motivate them or create a poor culture within your building. It is important that you define people's work, but then allow them to do their jobs. Many leaders, including myself, have worked for micromanagers who did not allow employees to really work to their strengths. In this type of environment, it is very easy for people to sit back and wait to be instructed to accomplish a task for fear of being "wrong" or being criticized or reprimanded by the leader. The best type of leadership model is a "loose-tight" leadership model. In this model, individuals are given the autonomy to use their judgment and make decisions to improve the organization. The leader establishes frequent check-in opportunities with key leaders to monitor the progress of work and to provide continued direction. It is very inspiring and motivating to work for a leader who believes in you, understands your strengths, and challenges you to utilize your strengths and continue to grow. This is the type of leader you should become. This section will offer you a few tips to consider as you work with your staff.

How You Will Model a Value System for Your School

Your staff members will treat each other the way you treat them or allow them to treat one another. As you think about your first hundred days, think about ways you can explicitly communicate and model behaviors that you expect. One way that you can achieve this is to identify a great book that illustrates what you expect and give each staff member a copy. You can use part of your staff meeting time or teacher collaboration time to highlight key aspects of the book or have someone facilitate reflection activities with your staff. A staff blog is also an effective way to reflect on written text. There are thousands of books that you can choose from that communicate a philosophy that connects to your mission or vision. At the end of this book, I have included a brief annotated bibliography with some favorites I have used or seen used effectively (see page 121).

People will listen to what you say, but they are going to pay much more attention to what you do. One of the burdens of leadership is that you become much more restricted in the things you can say or do as you move higher in the organizational hierarchy. Now that you are the principal, you have to be very cautious of your word choice, how often you interact with individuals and for what purposes, and what you openly accept and reject. Everything you do will be put under the strict scrutiny test, so use all of your actions as an opportunity to reaffirm your core beliefs.

If you expect teachers to be in your hallways during student transitions from one class to another, then you and your assistant principals should be in the hallways during transitions. If you are a stickler for people arriving to work and leaving on time, then you need to report on time and leave on time. If you expect people to stay engaged during meetings (for example, to stay off their Blackberry), then you need to stay engaged during meetings. If you expect assistant principals and leadership team members to frequently visit classrooms, then you need to frequently visit classrooms. By modeling what it is that you expect, you will motivate your staff to support your initiatives. People's sense of commitment will increase when they know that they are walking with the leader as opposed to being told to walk while the leader sits.

What You Celebrate Daily and Weekly

The first hundred days are symbolically your most significant days. These are the days that the most attention will be placed on you as you perform your duties for the first time. Each action and statement from you will affirm or reject what has traditionally been the norms of operation within your school. As such, it is important for you to think about what you are celebrating daily and weekly.

Daily celebrations are those actions, statements, or behaviors you reinforce with staff and students daily. They can be as simple as making the daily announcements and reinforcing your school's vision statement or mission statement at the end of each announcement. The positive reinforcement that you and your designees give staff for exhibiting specific behaviors is another form of daily celebration.

An example of a weekly celebration for me was recognizing staff members who committed to posting homework assignments online and updating their grades every two weeks online. My school used an online grading system in which grades were automatically posted for students and parents to see when teachers entered them; teachers could also upload homework assignments. This system was a great idea, but in practice, teachers had difficulty finding time to post homework daily, and many teachers did not consistently update grades every two weeks. Teachers were not required to upload homework assignments by their contract, so it was a difficult practice to enforce effectively. To recognize teachers who did adhere to our school expectations, students would fill out an index card during their lunch period each Thursday to identify the teacher who they felt helped them the most by uploading homework assignments and entering grades consistently. Then I or one of my assistant principals would review the cards and announce the winner on Friday, publicly expressing our thanks for the effort to help students. The parent association provided funds to give the teacher a gift card. This practice was a nonthreatening, fun way to reinforce a schoolwide expectation and keep it at the forefront of the staff and the community's mind.

Think of all of the fun activities you can do to show appreciation of staff and celebrate positive behaviors within your building. Here are a few additional ideas that can help you think of others.

- ◆ Verbally acknowledge a staff member each week on the morning announcements in a Caught Ya' Demonstrating Excellence Program. Identify what the staff members did and give them a balloon, banner, and/or gift card to thank them publically.

- ◆ At staff meetings, make it a practice to have staff members write thank-you cards to someone who has helped them. Create a hall display of these thank-you notes and change it monthly.

- ◆ Develop a system and devote time on your schedule to write at least one commendation per week to a staff member. (See Figure 2.8.) Acknowledge the teacher in your staff bulletin or newsletter. Require other administrators and department chairs to write commendations as well and keep track of who is acknowledged.

Figure 2.8 Sample Commendation Letter to a Staff Member

Memorandum

To: Teacher A
From: Shawn Joseph, Ed.D., Principal
Subject: Fantastic Job

I want to recognize you for demonstrating excellent teaching skills during our recent guest observers' walk-throughs. I also wanted to commend you for your efforts to train staff at our last staff meeting. Your session on the components of culturally responsive teaching was well received.

During the walk-throughs, the observers recognized that students were actively manipulating the electronic whiteboard. Students were having fun and learning! It was evident that they use it often based upon their ease with it. It was clear that students understood what was expected of them, and the objectives were clear and written at the mastery level. You continuously checked for understanding, and when students seemed confused, you retaught the concept while giving students who had mastered the concept another activity to do that would engage and challenge them. You spoke predominantly in Spanish to students.

Utopia High School is a great place to work and learn because we have caring teachers like you. Once again, nice job!

Cc: School file

◆ Create schoolwide competitions focusing on accomplishing specific behavior and celebrate the staff's and students' progression toward the goal. For example, hold a competition to see which grade level can receive the fewest discipline referrals per month. Chart each grade level's progress and have leading grade-level staff share a strategy that is working for them on the announcements, in newsletters, and on list-serves.

◆ Take time to write your staff weekly. Share positive stories about things that are happening in the building that are aligned with your school's vision. Your acknowledgement of staff members' personal stories shows that you are paying attention to what they are doing and it shows staff members what you value.

Just remember that as the principal, you are the culture keeper. If you are positive and energetic and you consistently promote and acknowledge the positive, you will have improved morale in your building. Moreover, teachers and students will be inspired to continue to work hard for you.

Summary

As principal, building a team that is motivated to do whatever it takes to ensure that all children are valued, inspired, and held to high expectations is one of your most important priorities. As a principal, you should begin the process by evaluating key members of your leadership team. It is better to make changes early in your tenure if they are necessary. The systems that you establish to work with, develop, and inspire your team will determine whether all children learn at high levels within your building.

Reflection Questions for Principals

1. What are your three or four priorities for your leadership team members?
2. What system will you put in place to monitor the quality of students' classroom work in your school?
3. How will you ensure that the observational process in your building is seamless if more than one observer is giving feedback to teachers?
4. How will you create a sense of urgency through the observation process by looking at student data and student work?
5. What programs will you implement to motivate and celebrate employees?

Reflection Questions and Activities for Prospective Administrative Candidates

1. What are the leadership evaluation criteria utilized in your local school district? How would you prioritize the responsibilities?
2. What process is used to monitor the quality of classroom work in your school? Is it effective?
3. Describe how the feedback and observation process is executed in your current work location. Have you been stretched by design?
4. What are strategies that you have seen employed to motivate employees in your work location?

Timeline of Activities

July

- ♦ Read leadership team personnel files and their most recent evaluations.
- ♦ Meet individually with leadership team members.
- ♦ Review the evaluation criteria used for leadership development team members.

August

- ♦ Read teacher observations done by qualified observers in your school from the previous year.
- ♦ Assess how your leadership team members used their time prior to your arrival.
- ♦ Identify a book for your leadership team to study with you.
- ♦ Identify celebration activities and processes.

September

- ♦ Create the school's teacher classroom observation schedule.
- ♦ Communicate your leadership priorities to your leadership team in writing.
- ♦ Develop your leadership team's meeting schedule for the year, including individual check-in meetings with your leaders.
- ♦ Begin writing staff commendations.
- ♦ Begin weekly staff letter, bulletins, and e-mails.

October

- ♦ Give leadership team members feedback on their work.

3

Think Like a Mayor

Activities in this chapter support the following principal leadership standards:

Educational Leadership Policy Standards

➤ **ISSLC 2008 Standard 4:** Education leaders promote the success of every student by collaborating with faculty and community members, responding to diverse community interests and needs, and mobilizing community resources.

➤ **ISSLC 2008 Standard 6:** Education leaders promote the success of every student by understanding, responding to, and influencing the political, social, economic, legal, and cultural context.

National Board Core Propositions for Accomplished Educational Leaders

Accomplished educational leaders:

➤ model professional, ethical behavior and expect it from others

➤ advocate on behalf of their schools, communities, and profession

---

Processes for Meeting Your New Leadership Team Members, Staff, and Community

Transition plans are very important for new executives. Think about it. In most high-level government jobs, transition teams are developed to ensure that there is a seamless shift from one leader to the next. In schools, principals usually receive a note on the desk from the previous principal with the keys to the building and a file of things to do.

As the principal, you will need to take your destiny into your own hands and begin to think about how you are going to do some of the important work that lies ahead from the moment you walk into your office. If you are a new principal or future principal, you have inherited or will inherit a staff, the parents of your students, and a community. You need to get to know them quickly. If you are a veteran principal, you will also need to assess the dynamics of a new school year.

Most principals do not fully understand the political nature of the position. I know when I was appointed as a new principal, I was more concerned with understanding my school's culture and getting to know my teachers. I was totally oblivious to the politics involved in working with the parents, the staff, the central office, and the greater community. I was lucky that my community took mercy on me! In your first hundred days, like any other executive in business or public service, you will need to develop a hundred-day plan to embrace your constituency. If you are a new principal, this is your opportunity to actively assimilate into the culture of your community and simultaneously develop the brand of your school. If you are a veteran principal, plans need to be made to meet your new constituency. Whether your school currently has a good reputation in the community or not, you will need to make your rounds to create energy for supporting the children in your school. In this chapter, I'll offer some points of wisdom that will get you off to a terrific start.

Share Information About Yourself

At the beginning of the summer, you should immediately contact the person responsible for maintaining your school's Web site (assuming that your school has a Web site). Today, Web sites are an extremely popular medium of communication, and parents, staff, and students will be visiting it soon to get to know you. I'd recommend you include the following on the school Web site:

- ♦ A picture of you—make it a good one!

- ♦ A brief biography: let people know about your previous job experiences and some little known facts about you. If you are comfortable revealing personal information, let them know a bit about your family and your hobbies.

- ♦ Write a brief, half-page welcome letter letting them know how excited you are to serve them.

- ♦ Display a visual of your beliefs as they relate to education.

- ♦ Identify at least two dates for parents to visit you for a meet-and-greet. If possible, host one at school and one at a community location.

As parents read about you, view your picture, and learn about your beliefs, they will begin to get excited about your tenure. You should also contact your neighborhood's local reporter and arrange a meeting to discuss your plans for your school. It's usually big news to get a new principal in the neighborhood, and this is yet another way for parents, staff, and students to hear your thoughts. Veteran principals should contact media outlets to discuss your successes from the previous school year and upcoming school events. If you are in a school district where media coverage of schools tends to be negative or mostly investigative reporting, you should consult your district's media relations person if one is available. You don't want your good intentions to backfire on your school.

It is important to be cognizant of how you communicate with the media. I would also suggest that you consult a veteran principal who is familiar with your geographic region and who has experience working with the media, especially if your district does not have a media person you can contact for advice. As you communicate, I would caution you not to get caught in any traps set by reporters or others looking for gossip. It is very easy to link problems to your predecessor. Bad idea! Consciously sidestep any negative talk by focusing on your excitement to serve as the new principal and your enthusiasm for listening to your parents, staff, and students so you can collaboratively develop next steps to move your school to higher heights. Did that sound politically correct enough? Statements like "There are no challenges that we cannot overcome as a community" or "Today marks a new beginning for us as a school and we are going to work to make our school one of the best schools in the country" will keep your parents optimistic about your tenure. For veteran principals, every year marks a new beginning; it is important to remind your community of this reality.

As you meet with parents and communicate with your community, stay focused on one or two key messages like your desire to hear what has been working for your constituency or what improvement your constituents would like to see at the school. Again, your ability to demonstrate your willingness to listen will go a long way in making a good impression.

Build Relationships with Key Constituencies

I've discussed the need for you to assess your leadership team and to develop systems of accountability for them as you begin a new year as the principal. Your leadership team is one small aspect of the relationship building that needs to be done within the first hundred days. You need to create structures for you to communicate with parents, staff, and students. The more people hear from you, the more at ease they will be working with you when the school year begins. Let's look at ideas for each constituency group.

Meeting Parents

Parent meetings will vary from school to school as different communities have very different expectations. Proper protocol calls for you to make contact with the parent-association president or board, if your community has a parent association, as soon as you are appointed. Make it a point to learn the board members' names as quickly as possible and to give them an opportunity to share their perceptions of the school's strengths and areas for improvement. It is important in these first meetings that you listen and understand their perspectives. If you are a new principal, parents will most often express varying perspectives about your predecessor. They may have loved your predecessor and want you to build upon your predecessor's progress, or they may have hated your predecessor and expect you to be a change agent. A winning strategy for you in either case is to stay neutral and just listen. Don't get me wrong: it is important for you to understand what the perceptions were about your predecessor from the perspective of all stakeholders because this will have an impact on how you do what you will ultimately need to do. If you are listening carefully, you will get a good sense of the general "state of the union" and you'll be able to navigate without evoking your predecessor's spirit! All too often, new administrators try to earn political points by commenting, positively or negatively, on their predecessor's work. It is not wise or professional to do so, especially if your comments are negative. Those things that have worked well should be preserved in the immediate future; by doing so, you will be honoring your predecessor. Those things that need to change will be apparent as you listen to all of your constituencies. Look for similarities between the parents' perceptions and your staff's perceptions. Those are quick win areas for you as you decide which issues you will tackle first. If you are a veteran principal working with a new parent association board, you want to listen and work closely with your board to address or clarify any existing negative perceptions. Educating new parents about how your school operates and being honest about challenges will build trust with your new board.

As discussed in Chapter 1, you will want to begin engaging parents so you can understand their hopes and dreams for their children's education. You will also want to begin to let them know more about you and your core values. Here are some suggestions on how to gather information:

♦ On your school's Web site, create a link that allows parents to write a statement about their hopes and dreams for their children's education. Once parents submit the statement and hit send, direct the emails to you and the parent-association president.

Collate these statements and share them at parent-association meetings.

♦ Have your secretaries give parents feedback cards when they visit the main office. Have secretaries ask parents if they can take a moment to share their thoughts about what they want for their children this coming school year. Have someone enter the comments electronically into a database.

♦ Send directions to the feedback form online to parents via a newsletter. Let parents know that they can complete a form in the main office on their next visit if they prefer to write it instead of sending it electronically.

♦ One hour prior to Back-to-School Night, host a meet-and-greet offering food, music, and time to socialize. Allow parents access to school computers to share input or have them complete a feedback form and leave it with you.

♦ Conduct quarterly parent coffees at different times of the day. Use these opportunities to have unstructured dialogues with parents on topics of their interest.

♦ Collaborate with religious leaders in your community to host meet-and-greets before or after services at their organization's meeting location. At the event, pass out a list of upcoming important dates for the school.

♦ Set up a table at your local mall or supermarket to talk with parents and to pass out information about your school. This is a great activity for your public relations committee to spearhead if you develop one.

All of these ways will communicate to parents that you want to understand more about their wants and needs. These methods will give you a better understanding of the diversity of perspectives within your community as well!

Meeting Culture Brokers

Beyond the parent-association governance, which in many schools tends to be the well-to-do or politically savvy parents within the community, think about who the culture brokers are within your school. I define a culture broker as an individual who knows a lot about different aspects of your school community and is connected to a lot of people within a certain section of the community. Ask the outgoing principal, your central office supervisor, and your superintendent if they can share the names of influential families within your school community. Influence is wielded by people whom others within the community go to for information, advice, or direction. Who are the community members that other community members listen to when issues arise? You want to make contact with these individuals and invite them to the school or a local gathering place, like a coffee shop, because you want to know what they think about your school. Most principals schedule frequent times to meet with the parent association. You should also schedule frequent times to talk with culture brokers within your community as many may not actively participate in the parent association. Culture brokers may include the following individuals:

- Political figures within the community, such as county council members, state delegates, and local school-board members

- Religious leaders of all faiths

- Feeder pattern principal colleagues

- Little League coaches

- Boys' and girls' club managers

- Barbers and hair stylists

- Homeowner's association presidents and board members

- Apartment complex managers

- Local university admissions counselors and personnel

- Parents from ethnically diverse backgrounds who have had children in the district for years at various schooling levels

- Chamber of commerce boards

- Local government department heads

- Key teachers or support professionals like secretaries, building services workers, and others who work in your building

It is important for you to identify potential culture brokers early on each year. Notice that this list does not just include people whose children attend your school. People do not need to have children in your school to discuss your school in a positive or a negative light. In addition, people's educational background or knowledge about schools is not very important. What is important is their role in influencing others.

Culture brokers may not frequent the school. Once you have identified some key individuals who have the capacity to influence key constituencies about your school, you may need to visit them to introduce yourself and open lines of communication. Here are some ways to stay connected with culture brokers who may not visit the school frequently:

- Give them a schedule of events that will be held at the school, and send them a reminder as events approach during the school year. If it is appropriate, acknowledge their presence when they attend events. Public figures love being acknowledged.

- Include them on your distribution lists for telephone messages, e-mail messages, or newsletters. Ask them to share or post information in their newsletters or weekly communications with their constituency if appropriate.

- If school board policies permit, include a sponsor section on your school's Web site, including various culture brokers' business information and a link to their Web site.

- Honor community members and volunteers quarterly, and include culture brokers in the celebration for their support.

- Be sure that they have your e-mail address and your telephone number so they can call you if they need to ask you anything or clarify community concerns.

- Be sure your public relations committee is in contact with these individuals throughout the year. You should have some of the committee representatives with you when you meet with the culture brokers.

You will discover that culture brokers will come and go from your school, so you must constantly be in search of them and build a positive, substantive relationship in order to gain their support for school initiatives. As you increase the venues in which communication about the school is disseminated, you will increase levels of trust and build strong support for your school.

Meeting Teachers and Staff

As I stated previously, from the first moment you walked into your office, you created anxiety at some level within your building if you are a new principal. You want to reduce this anxiety by having some face-to-face time with staff as soon as possible. Schedule one or two social events over the summer for staff to meet-and-greet you. Food and music are always great icebreakers. It is convenient to have these events at your school, but sometimes an alternative venue, like a local restaurant, bowling party, or sporting event, can create opportunities for more informal dialogue.

As you prepare for such an event, keep in mind that people want to know that you care before they want to hear what you expect. If you have created a graphic showing your belief statement and vision of teaching, as described in Chapter 1, this is a great time to take a few minutes to discuss your core beliefs. When you attend these events, spend more time listening to people and observing dynamics than talking! You can learn a lot at these events.

Hiring New Staff

Nothing says more about who you are as a leader than who you choose to keep around you as members of your leadership team and who you hire. Nothing! One lesson principals must learn early is that it is not about you— it's about the team you assemble. Usually, principals have opportunities to fill teaching and nonteaching vacancies over the summer. I will give you some advice on filling teaching vacancies, though nonteaching vacancies are critical in a building as well!

Some of the best advice I received about hiring new staff is that a teacher's moral character, will, and drive to help children succeed are as important as content knowledge. Let's face it—your staff will be the ambassadors of the school to your community. As the leader of the school, you need to know that you have assembled a team that understands the moral urgency of ensuring a high-level education for all students. Each individual interaction that staff members have with students and with the community will define the tone and the perceptions people have of your school. What message do you want future staff members to communicate? How do you know the hearts of your new hires? Here are some questions that may help you delve into your new hires' educational philosophies that define who they are as educational leaders.

Questions for Educators with Previous Educational Experience

- ◆ Why did you become an educator?
- ◆ If I were to call your last employer and ask her to share the legacy you are leaving at the school, what would she say?
- ◆ Share with us a famous person whom you admire more than any other celebrity. Why do you value this person so much? How do the person's attributes connect to your work with children?

- Identify a book, movie, or a combination of both that best describes your life's journey.

- How has your life's journey affected your interactions with the students you serve?

- Why do you believe the achievement gap exists, and what can you do about it as a teacher with the children in your classroom?

- What does equity mean to you?

- What are some challenges associated with ensuring equity and excellence?

- As a teacher, what steps have you taken to overcome challenges of ensuring equity and excellence?

- What does a "whatever it takes" approach to teaching look like in a classroom?

- If I were to call your previous employer, would he describe you as a "whatever it takes" teacher?

As a hiring manager, you will probably find that interviewing teachers with previous experience is easy. These individuals come to the interview with a history that can be researched. Never hire experienced candidates without checking their references. Experienced teachers' history is a great window into what they potentially will do at your school. If you are lucky, you will have an opportunity to interview and hire candidates with a track record of commitment, compassion, and excellence. If you can't find a veteran, you will need to hire and support new teaching candidates.

Questions for New Teachers

- Why are you choosing to become an educator?

- Give me three examples of personal characteristics that will make you an outstanding educator.

- Why do you believe some students achieve while others fail? What can you do about this discrepancy as an educator?

- Share with us a famous person whom you admire more than any other celebrity. Why do you value this person?

- Describe a challenge you've faced in life, and discuss how you overcame it.

Figure 3.1 Sample Letter to Potential Staff Members

COUNTY PUBLIC SCHOOLS

Utopia Elementary School

12348 Nowhere Road • Anyplace, USA 00000 • (123) 234-5678

Office of the Principal

Date:

Teaching is one of the most important and rewarding professions in the world! At Utopia Elementary School, we are seeking outstanding educators to assist us in our quest to provide a world-class education to the children and the families we serve. The candidates that we will select for the _____ school year will possess the following characteristics:

♦ Demonstrate a passion for equity and excellence: We are interested in candidates who set high standards for themselves and their students. More importantly, we are seeking people who see teaching as "social activism": people who are committed to effectively captivating, inspiring, and teaching our children at high levels.

♦ Demonstrate a commitment to collaboration: We have mountains to move here at Utopia Elementary School. However, we believe we can move mountains by working with each other, our students' parents, our business community, and most importantly, our students.

♦ Demonstrate a commitment to reflective practice: Each year poses new challenges for us as a school. We service an extremely diverse range of learners, and we are always challenging ourselves to look at our own practices and change for the better! There is never a time in which we have "learned enough," and we seek people who are comfortable in a highly dynamic, continually changing environment!

♦ Demonstrate a commitment to professionalism: We take customer satisfaction seriously as a school. Our customers include our staff, our students, our students' parents, our Utopia Elementary School community, and our business community. We are seeking people who understand how to create win-win scenarios by balancing personal wants and the interests of our customers.

♦ Demonstrate a commitment to building high-quality relationships: We believe significant learning does not occur without a significant relationship. We place an enormous emphasis on

---

building meaningful, respectful relationships between staff, parents, and students.

This has been an extraordinary year of learning for us as a community. We are looking forward to identifying individuals with similar ideals and characteristics as we move forward on our journey toward excellence.

If you believe that the characteristics that have been described reflect who you are as a person and as an educator, we would love to speak with you. Please free to e-mail me at _____ or call me directly at _____. As a faculty member, you will understand why we say "Excellence is our priority at Utopia Elementary School."

Sincerely,

Principal

♦ As you think about your own K–12 educational experience, describe your best teacher. What made this teacher so good?

♦ Describe how your classroom will look and discuss your rationale for your design.

♦ What is the role of children's parents in their education, and what will you do as a teacher to work with families?

♦ What has been your experience with families of different cultural backgrounds?

♦ What steps will you take to ensure effective communication with people of different cultural backgrounds?

♦ What steps will you take to inspire unmotivated students?

♦ What steps will you take to build substantive relationships with your students?

These sample questions will give you some insight into the character and disposition of your new hires as they begin to conceptualize their roles as teachers. At the end of this chapter, I have included a sample letter that can be customized to introduce your school's core values to potential new hires. (See Figure 3.1.)

Meeting with Students

The most important constituency you need to meet and connect with is your student constituency. Your students are the reason you have a job. It is your job to influence staff to have a dramatic impact on students' achievement. You also have a huge responsibility directly impacting students through your words and actions. If you are successful in inspiring your students to achieve greatness, your parents, staff, and community will immediately fall in love, and you will be a local legend! Unfortunately, this is easier said than done, so the following are some suggestions to help you. I will give advice for secondary students and then advice for elementary students.

Secondary Students

The students you will need to connect with immediately are your upper classmen. In a middle school, your eighth graders will determine your success in year one, and in a high school, your senior class will make or break you. As the principal, you will have this group of students for the shortest amount of time. Typically, the upperclassmen dictate the culture of the school building. Here are four suggestions to get them on your side quickly.

On the first day of school, start the day off by meeting with your upperclassmen before they go to their first-period class. This is your opportunity to welcome them and to let them know that you value them and plan on having a productive year. At this meeting, establish a tone by letting them know about your core values; share their performance data with them from the previous year; set clear academic targets for them to achieve, like increasing the number of students who make the honor roll by a certain percent; discuss activities that you have planned for them as the leaders of the school. In this way, you are sending multiple key messages about your desire to connect with them, your academic expectations, and the rewards you plan for them as the seniors of the building.

In addition, structure your schedule to meet with each grade-level class. You can follow the same basic format for each meeting, but you will need to change the overall tenor based upon the grade-level. Ninth graders, for example, need to learn about the nuances of the high-school experience. Tenth and eleventh graders need to understand the importance of the grade point average (GPA) and preparing for college exams (you might want to create GPA and SAT/ACT targets and discuss schoolwide incentives for all students who achieve the target).

Next, you will need to put structures in place to communicate with your students frequently. (1) If your school has a school newspaper, speak with the editor about having a standing principal's section. (2) In addition, schedule cafeteria time at least once a week to have informal dialogue with random students. (3) Schedule a standing meeting with student government representatives throughout the school year. (4) Attend your school's major sporting events (at least until the half-time show for the first year). (5) Schedule grade-level honor roll achievement talks. (6) Schedule focus groups to talk with underperforming students at the midquarter mark and at the end of the quarter.

Lastly, to monitor the pulse of what is happening from your students' perspective, you should schedule quarterly focus group meetings with your students. During your first year, I would include more upperclassmen in the focus group meetings, so they are aware that you are listening to them. These are great opportunities to gather information about what is working and what is not working for the students. Once you gather the information, let them know via their newspaper, cafeteria time, your blog, and/or the morning announcements that you have heard what they have to say.

Elementary Students

Elementary students tend to be much more open and receptive to listening versus the typical secondary student. As in the secondary school, it will be important for you to build a strong rapport with your upper grade-level students first. Your primary students will know only your influence! At the elementary level, your visual acknowledgements of their excellence and high expectations are important. Here are some suggestions for you to consider as you think of the power of your influence on your students.

♦ Create bulletin boards with pictures of your students displayed. Ask your students' parents to identify a college they would like their child to attend and place the name of the college under each picture.

♦ Ensure that there is a variety of student work displayed throughout your building. During the morning announcements, be sure to highlight different pieces of student work you have read to let students know that you value high-quality work.

♦ Walk through classrooms daily and speak with students about what they are working on in class. Give students specific affirmation when you see progress.

♦ Schedule monthly achievement celebrations for students and invite their parents to attend. The achievement celebrations can focus on your school's core values in addition to academic achievements.

- Schedule monthly meetings with the student association to get feedback from your upper-grade students.

- Schedule meetings with your safety patrol. They generally see and hear everything!

Be Visible

One of the most powerful actions that you can take as a principal is to simply be visible. This sounds easier than it actually is in action. Your staff, parents, and students want to know that you are around. They also want to know that you know what is happening in your building. It is very easy for a principal to be locked away in an office. Most school districts give principals enough work to do to keep them locked away for at least ten hours a day. As I discussed earlier, you are the PRINCIPAL. Your job is to make sure things get done.

I know many principals who pride themselves on having an open-door policy. They tell staff that their door is always open. As a result, parents, students, and staff feel free to drop by to chat about issues. If you take this personal management style on, you are destining yourself to fourteen- to sixteen-hour days. People will continue to take up your time, and you will not be very efficient or effective in getting your work done.

I can still remember my first year as a new principal. To say I was overwhelmed would be an understatement. I was drowning in an ocean of papers, expectations, and impromptu visits by staff, parents, and students. I still remember the dreaded in-box/out-box that was on my desk. Daily, I watched my secretary drop items into the in-box that I was supposed to read or respond to, but I just couldn't find a way to move items from the in-box to the out-box! I am thankful to a colleague who had been a very successful principal who happened to have a daughter attending my school. His sage advice altered my thinking as a principal, and it allowed me to become much more effective as I thought about my role and what was really important as I managed day-to-day operations.

The prime point to remember is that other people in your building should be dealing with most of the paperwork that your district requires you to do. The reality is that there is very little, other than budgetary items, observations, and evaluations, that you as the principal cannot assign someone else to do. Most of the time-consuming actions that need to be done could be handled by a knowledgeable secretary, assistant principal, or teacher leader. You will need to develop efficiency systems to ensure that the work gets done. As you distribute leadership, you will be able to have a greater presence within your school community.

First, you should consider meeting with your secretary every day for an hour. This will be the most important time of your day if done right. During this time, have your secretary read and summarize all the memos and actions you need to know about. If there are actions that need to be done, determine who should complete them. If a designee is to complete the action, have your secretary schedule a time on your calendar prior to the due date for you to review the item before it is submitted.

In addition, allow your secretary to read and respond to your e-mails. Reading e-mail is, by far, one of the most time-consuming activities of the principalship in many parts of the country. However, most of the actions that are needed will require you as principal to set up a meeting or a phone call or to redirect the e-mail writer to someone else. These are all things that a secretary can do. Think about it. If you meet with your secretary daily, can't she just tell you whom she has scheduled meetings with on your behalf and the nature of the issues? If a parent wants to discuss a teacher issue, for example, the secretary can log on as you and assure the parent that the issue is of great concern to you. Then she could say that the grade-level administrator or a counselor will contact the parent to resolve the situation. She could also let the parent know that you have scheduled a follow-up call to see whether the parent is satisfied with the outcome of the situation. A personal follow-up call is much less time-consuming than spending hours addressing the issue.

For this system to work, you need to have a competent secretary who understands your expectations about customer service and who has good judgment about assigning items to the appropriate staff member and following up on all items. Giving up e-mail is difficult for some administrators, but remember, there were great principals prior to e-mail! Even if you don't give up e-mail right away, you should definitely give up reading memos. Trust your secretary to update you. If she cannot do it, you probably need a new secretary.

Finally, papers that need your signature should be signed and taken away by the secretary. You don't need an in-box/out-box. Your secretary should bring items in for your meeting, and they should go with her at the conclusion of the meeting.

These simple, practical tips will give you more time to do what is most important: be out and about among the school community. Consider the following additional suggestions:

- Have your secretary schedule you into classrooms weekly. These occasions are your priority; schedule other appointments around these times. In addition, have your secretary schedule your meetings with groups of teachers at team planning times, department times, or individual conferences. You can also schedule specific occasions for you to attend student government meetings or talk to students in the cafeteria. Your schedule will be full, but it will be a schedule that you have intentionally designed to allow you to meet the people you need to talk to in your building.

- Plan to speak on your morning announcements at least three times per week. Think strategically about a data point that you can briefly discuss at least once per week (e.g., enrollment data in a targeted intervention, discipline data, homework completion data, or grade-level reading log data).

- Stand at the front entrance to greet students, staff, and parents each morning as they enter the building, and in the afternoon at dismissal.

- During each transition at the secondary level, work with your administrators and your security team to walk each section of the building to encourage students to make it to class on time. Acknowledge teachers and staff who are at their doors supporting hallway monitoring.

- If you have an automated telephone system, call parents and staff weekly to give them an update of upcoming school events. Post your message on your Web site, and send it out on a school list-serve.

- Attend all parent-association meetings and board of directors' meetings. Give your community a written report including staff and student accomplishments for the month, student referral data, upcoming events, and quarterly honor-roll data.

By employing these suggestions, you will establish a clear, visible presence in the lives of your staff, parents, and students.

Pay Attention to the Polls

It is very easy for a principal to become engrossed in the work of running a school. Although the principalship is not technically a political job, principals fail when they do not keep track of the school community's perceptions of the principal's leadership. Clearly, it is not healthy or wise for any leader to chase "poll" numbers. Leaders need to stand for what is morally right, and there are times when what is morally right is not politically right. However, all public leaders, including principals, need to be constantly aware of the politics and perceptions of their actions. The politics and perceptions of a principal's work will dictate how the morally difficult work will be executed effectively on behalf of children. Here are some suggestions to keep you aware of the perceptions of your constituency:

- Facilitate quarterly meetings with small groups of faculty beginning the first quarter of the school year. Have small groups of staff rotate through to talk with you throughout the day. I suggest having food and drinks at this meeting. During the meeting, have faculty provide feedback on key changes or actions you have made. Allow participants to provide anonymous feedback in writing at the meeting in addition to speaking with you directly.

- Collate and share the feedback that you have received from parents via parent-association meetings, e-mail, or a survey. If you have not received much feedback, distribute feedback forms via your newsletter, your phone message system if you have one, and major quarterly events such as concerts. Simply ask, "What is working and what would you like me to improve?"

- Collect feedback from your students quarterly. Again, simple qualitative data is very meaningful for you. Conduct a random sampling of homerooms in your school and ask students to identify an upgrade to school processes and something that is working for them.

Once you have the data from all three of these groups, share the information openly with your leadership team and your parent association or board of directors. Look for themes in your responses. Publicly share perceived common successes, and acknowledge and discuss common areas of concern. Once people know you are listening to them, acknowledging their concerns, and discussing next steps, they will be open to working with you.

Seemingly small process changes can turn into political disasters if you do not work with your parents, staff, and students. Always think of ways to gather feedback and make adjustments based upon collaborating with your stakeholders. By openly acknowledging the feelings of constituents, creating work committees, creating timelines to evaluate the process, continuing to solicit feedback on the process, and making adjustments as necessary, you will allow your constituencies to see that they have a voice and that you are willing to heed their voice and work with them in order to achieve a common goal.

As a principal, your ability to listen, reflect, and make adjustments to achieve common goals will take you much further than your ability to take charge and make unilateral decisions.

Summary

As a principal, you will have lots to reflect upon. You will not work in a vacuum; indeed, you will work with many constituencies to achieve your goals. Take time to communicate to your constituencies who you are as a leader. Take time to understand whom you are serving. You'll begin building valuable relationships with your constituencies by listening to them and taking time to have frequent communication with them. As you collect feedback from your constituencies by design, you will stay in front of issues that might otherwise create negative perceptions of your leadership.

Reflection Questions for Principals

1. What are your three most essential core values, and how will you communicate them to your school community?
2. Who are the culture brokers in your community, and what structures will you put in place to communicate with them effectively and frequently?
3. What steps have you taken to be visible within your school community?
4. What processes have you put in place to gather feedback on your work in the school community?
5. What resources will you need to establish a relationship with all facets of your community?

Reflection Questions and Activities for Prospective Administrative Candidates

1. What strategies did your principal use to get to know about you? How were the principal's priorities communicated?
2. Identify the culture brokers within your school community.
3. What strategies would you utilize to be visible within your school community?

4. What mechanisms would you put in place to understand the perceptions about your leadership style within your school community?
5. Are there any unique challenges within your school community that would create a barrier to your effectively building relationships between your school and the community?

Timeline of Activities

July

♦ Update the school Web site.

♦ Write welcome letter to parents and staff.

♦ Complete graphic display of beliefs.

♦ Schedule meet-and-greets with parents and the community.

♦ Schedule a designated time to meet with your secretary daily.

August

♦ Begin to identify culture brokers and begin scheduling meetings.

♦ Place feedback cards in the main office and on the school Web site.

♦ Set after-school activities calendar.

♦ Schedule monthly achievement events for students.

September

♦ Begin weekly automated calls to parents if available.

♦ Begin monthly web messages, blogs, Twitter messages.

♦ Begin meetings with student groups.

♦ Solicit feedback at Back-to-School Night.

♦ Visit malls, places of worship, supermarkets, and gathering places with public relations committee.

October

♦ Continue identifying and meeting culture brokers.

♦ Continue visiting malls, places of worship, supermarkets, and gathering places with public relations committee.

Party Like a Data Rock Star

Activities in this chapter support the following principal leadership standards:

Educational Leadership Policy Standards
➢ **ISLLC 2008 Standard 2:** Education leaders promote the success of every student by advocating, nurturing, and sustaining a school culture and instructional program conducive to student learning and staff professional growth.
National Board Core Propositions for Accomplished Educational Leaders
➢ Accomplished educational leaders drive, facilitate, and monitor the teaching and learning process.

"Leadership is second only to classroom instruction among all school-related factors that contribute to what students learn at school" (Leithwood, Louis, Anderson, & Wahlstrom, 2004, p. 1). As principal, your leadership, particularly in the area of data monitoring, is extremely important. Our era demands that all schools discuss "data," and plans for improving "data" are commonplace. In your first hundred days as principal, you will need to know which data is most important and how to get your staff to think about their classroom data. In this chapter, I am going to discuss your role as the "data leader" in your school. However, it is important to take a moment to comment on the moral imperative of our work in this area.

First of all, the "data" that we are discussing is so much more than quantifiable numbers. Data is about individual children and individual lives. Within the pie graphs, bar charts, and percentages are the hopes, dreams, and aspirations of real families. We are considered a great nation, and in comparison to the opportunities afforded to citizens of other nations, we are very blessed and fortunate to live in America. Even so, our nation has left generations behind based upon issues associated with race, class, socio-economic status, ethnicity, and gender. While a quality education has liberated thousands of individuals from being stuck at the bottom of a caste-like system, access to a quality education is still very unequal based upon one's zip code. As a result, throughout America, "data" generally looks good in those parts of the country with a commitment to investing in a quality education, but in areas with high concentrations of poverty, high concentrations of

African American and Hispanic children, and high concentrations of English as a second language students, we have seen "data" that is shameful for our nation. It has been said that a quality education is an inalienable civil right and that the next civil rights movement will address inequities in educational opportunities. All citizens, especially our nation's principals, should stand up to end the separate-but-equal policies that still exist in this country.

Your job as the data leader in your building is the same whether or not your school system has developed a sophisticated data warehouse system that puts classroom data at your fingertips. Don't get me wrong: if you have the tools to be able to pull up your teachers' classroom data from your computer, the work is much easier, but here I will discuss how you should think about your data from the perspective of a principal who does not have access to a data warehouse system. If you have a data warehouse system in your school district, the concepts that I will describe are still applicable.

Starting from the Basics

In the current era of accountability schools find themselves in, teachers, administrators, policymakers, and parents are all focused on one thing: student achievement. Whether you agree or disagree with the merits of such a narrow focus, I'm sure that you will agree that increasing student achievement for all children must be your focus as the learning leader of your building.

Here are a couple definitions that will be helpful to you as we move through this section of our discussion:

♦ Trailing indicator/summative data/lagging data: These terms, used interchangeably in the literature on school strategic planning, refer to school data that is an "after-the-fact" measure of learning. This data is reported after students' cumulative performance has been evaluated. Scores on SAT or ACT tests, annual state tests, district- or school-level unit assessments, and test like NAEP are all examples of trailing indicators/summative data/lagging data. This type of information is important in that it allows you to understand the degree to which learning has occurred at a given point in time.

♦ Leading indicators/formative data/leading data: These terms, also used interchangeably in the literature, refer to the data that you collect "along the way" before you obtain your lagging data.

In essence, the formative data is the data that determines the lagging data.

As a veteran or future principal, you need to understand that results will be obtained by developing systems to monitor and affect leading indicators at the classroom level. As soon as teachers return to your building to start the school year, you should sit down with teacher leaders to determine by department or grade level (1) what formative data will be monitored, (2) how formative data will be monitored, and (3) what are the processes and structures for reteaching and reassessing.

The Process of Monitoring Leading Indicators

School districts around the country have begun to invest heavily in creating assessments to measure the attainment of curricular outcomes. More advanced school districts are utilizing data warehouses—information technology systems that store, organize, and report data—to give administrators and teachers information about students' learning. While I believe this technology is helpful to building-level administrators and central office administrators who want to monitor results of schools, I have not seen such systems utilized by teachers to impact daily instruction. More often than not, by the time teachers receive data reports on formative assessment data utilizing a data warehouse, it is too late to inform their daily instruction.

Teaching is a very dynamic process. Since the era of accountability began, teachers have been overwhelmed with data collection and data analysis. In many districts, curricular demands force teachers to move at a rapid pace in order to expose students to all the content that is required for yearly testing. This has led to less time for teachers to reteach and reassess concepts that their students have not mastered. My advice to you is to utilize the expertise of your staff to ensure that teachers have real-time interventions based upon real-time data. To accomplish this goal, the teachers who are closest to the students need to determine what formative assessments will be utilized and the processes for reteaching and reassessing. This is a critical process that needs to be thoroughly understood. Here are some suggestions to guide your thinking:

♦ Meet with each of your teacher leaders to determine the precreated data points that are used in the subject areas or grade levels in your school. Often, textbooks or curriculum programs come with precreated assessments. School districts also create their own data points.

Figure 4.1 Collaborative Planning Expectations

The following are the expectations for grade-level teachers to use for their weekly planning.

Planning for Instruction and Assessment

1. Meet at least once per week using school collaborative planning time that has been created in your schedule. If your team prefers to meet before or after school, contact the principal for approval.
2. Map out a unit of study on a calendar with common pacing and common assessments.
3. Develop an assessment calendar for your unit of study. How many assessments will the team administer for each assessment objective?
4. Write common formative assessments.
5. Plan for new or different instructional strategies.
6. Share instructional materials and strategies with your colleagues.
7. Preview an upcoming formative or summative assessment to identify implications for instruction.

Assessing the Learning

1. Analyze common formative assessment data and plan for reteaching, reassessing, and changes in instruction.
2. Analyze student work following a protocol.
3. Grade common formative assessments together to ensure agreement in proficiency.

♦ Determine whether these data points are administered frequently enough to give teachers information about how students are progressing on the written and taught curricula.

♦ Charge your leadership team to meet with classroom teachers to (1) decide how often students will be assessed and (2) identify a process for creating common, teacher-made assessments to measure students' mastery of the written and the taught curricula. In many small schools, this will be your responsibility as the principal!

♦ Create a time for teachers to work together to create assessments and discuss data generated from the taught curricula.

♦ Clearly communicate expectations for collaborative planning. (See Figure 4.1).

As educators, we generally do not challenge our students to utilize their metacognitive skills. One way to do this and simultaneously generate data that can be used to improve weekly instruction is to develop a feedback tool that can be used with students. So what does this practice look like in operation? The practice I will describe focuses on two simultaneous processes occurring. The first process is a group process involving teachers of similar subject areas or grade levels. The second process involves individual teachers in their classrooms and their frequent monitoring of their own students' performance.

Group Process

First, the principal needs to identify a time when subject teachers or grade-level teachers can collaborate. Depending upon the level and structure of the school, this may occur during the school day or after school. Ideally, teachers will have time to collaborate at least twice per week for at least forty-five minutes to an hour. Even in American high schools, which have been described as islands of isolation, time can be found by earmarking it in the master schedule or utilizing department or faculty meeting time after school. We demonstrate our commitment to teachers' professionalism and collaboration by giving teachers adequate time to do this important work.

In addition, common assessments must be issued. Subject-area teams, or grade-level teams at the elementary level, need to determine how many common assessments will be created per quarter of school to assess the taught curriculum. Common assessments should be determined before instruction. This is extremely important. It sets the expectation for teachers, and it also allows for teacher input into the process. Once you have established how many assessments will be administered and you have a process for developing the common assessments, your job is to support teachers' work so that it is done effectively. Teachers need to start with the final outcomes in mind and teach students how to achieve those outcomes.

You and/or your designees should have copies of the common assessments that are going to be used to assess students each quarter. As principal, your job and your designees' jobs will be to facilitate discussions and expectations for next steps based on this data.

General questions that can be used to facilitate these discussions include:

♦ How did your class perform on common assessment #1 as compared to the classes of Teacher B and Teacher C?

♦ What did proficiency look like on this assessment? Describe the range-finding process you utilized with your colleagues.

- What did you and the other teachers discuss as possible root causes of the discrepancy in performance (if there was a discrepancy worth noting)?

- Based upon the analysis of data and the discussions you had with the other teachers, how did you reteach and reassess your students?

- What supports do you need to improve this data?

It is essential to have a facilitator lead any data discussions. The facilitator ensures that the discussion does not turn into a self-pity party or a guilt/blame game. The goal of looking at data together is to try to identify any best practices, trends, or next steps. When teachers know that you are holding them accountable for collaborating regarding their students' performance, they will change their practices and take more ownership of their data. Your job as principal is to support them in their efforts by providing the resources, the time, and the staff development that they need to achieve improved goals. One warning is this: do not take for granted that your teachers know how to collaborate. You, a member of your staff, an instructional specialist, or an outside consultant may need to work with your staff on how to do this. Just creating the time and expectation for collaboration to occur is a great start, but there is a lot of heavy lifting in between the start of this process and improved achievement.

Individual Data Process

Collaborating with subject-area colleagues to look at student data is important, but nothing is more important for teachers than to have systems in place to review and analyze individual student data. Ideally, teachers have a process in place to monitor how students perform on mastery objectives on a daily basis. Data such as exit cards and informal student assessments would be used daily and monitored. This is a daunting task for even the best of teachers.

When students are not learning, real-time interventions are needed. The only way to do this is to have tools and a classroom system to ensure that this process is occurring. The principal is a key figure in articulating this expectation and working with staff members to ensure that effective systems are in place. Here is an example of what a system might look like in a school.

At Utopia Middle School, the math department decided that it would gather input from students weekly and utilize the students' narrative data to plan for the following week. The team members decided as a group, in

Figure 4.2 Week in Review Sheet

Name: _____ Date: _____

Here are some things I have done in algebra this week:

1.   4.

2.   5.

3.   6.

Here are some things I have learned:

1.

2.

3.

4.

5.

I am most proud of my work on_____

_____

because_____

_____

Next week I plan to work on _____

_____

This week I enjoyed/did not enjoy when Dr. Joseph _____

Family comments:_____

_____

_____

I have read and discussed this evaluation with my child.

Signature _____ Date: _____

Figure 4.3 Protocol for Examining Student Work

Introduction: **5 minutes**

❑ Facilitator briefly introduces goals and guidelines for
  examining student work.

Teacher presentation: **5 minutes**

❑ Teacher-presenter describes the context for student work
  (assignment, scoring rubric).
❑ Teacher refers to the indicator being addressed.
❑ Teacher-presenter poses focusing question for feedback.

Clarifying questions: **5 minutes**

❑ Participants ask brief clarifying questions.

Examination of student work samples: **10 minutes**

❑ Samples of student work might be originals or photocopies.
❑ While examining student work, participants may think about:
    ◆ the strengths of the student
    ◆ the needs of the student
    ◆ what was interesting or surprising about this student work

Feedback: **8 minutes**

❑ Participants share feedback while teacher is silent.
❑ Facilitator may remind participants of focusing question.

Reflection: **5 minutes**

❑ Teacher-presenter speaks to comments or questions.
❑ Participants are silent.

Debrief: **2 minutes**

❑ Facilitator leads an open discussion of the experience the
  group has shared: What was effective? What concerns
  did the process raise?

---

collaboration with their principal, that they would meet each Friday before school. In return, the principal did not assign them an instructionally related activity block during the school day as he was able to do under contract language. On Thursday of each week, all math teachers issued students a "Week in Review" sheet to summarize their lessons from the previous Friday through that Thursday. (See Figure 4.2, page 89, for a copy of this sheet.) The Week in Review sheet identified what students had learned from Friday through Thursday. It also asked students to share what they were most proud of accomplishing academically during the week and to provide feedback to the teacher. Students could also comment on the classroom environment during the week. Similarly, students could share something that they enjoyed during the course of the week. Finally, there was a section where parents could comment after reviewing the sheet. Students submitted the sheets to the teachers at the beginning of class on Fridays. During the teachers' planning period, they reviewed the sheets with their colleagues, analyzing data to see if common themes emerged regarding students' likes or areas of difficulty. Teachers would use this feedback as part of their Friday morning planning. Teachers also had an opportunity during this time to discuss pedagogy that was used during the week that supported or challenged students' learning.

In this example, the tool was the weekly review sheet. All math teachers in the building used the same tool. The tool was designed and implemented by the teachers. If adjustments were made, they were done at a department meeting gathering feedback from all the math teachers. What makes this system effective is that it is understandable, is consistent, and addresses needs from the students' perspective. The teachers would collect exit cards or other means of assessment during the week to verify information that students shared. This additional student information is quick and easy for teachers to read, analyze, and use to change their instruction. Systems do not need to be complicated to be effective!

As a future principal or a new principal, you will need to work with your designees who are responsible for giving feedback to teachers in order to effectively ensure that group data analysis and individual data analysis are occurring. Together, these systems will have a dramatic effect on the focus and effectiveness of teaching and learning within school buildings. A sample data protocol has been included at the end of this chapter. (See Figure 4.3).

Creating a Sense of Urgency

Another important job of the principalship is to create a sense of urgency for quality teaching and quality learning. The tenets of quality teaching can be seen quite visibly as you develop systems to observe classrooms formally and informally. However, knowing whether quality learning is taking place involves a much more intentional, focused process. If you want to ultimately focus your school's efforts on learning, then you must have data conversations with your teachers frequently.

One of the most effective ways to accomplish this is to focus your post-observation conferences around evidence of student learning. As we know, there are lots of excellent presenters in classrooms who are not producing great results. One difficulty with how observations are conducted in many districts is that the postobservation conference discussion centers around observable actions and feedback on a lesson that was observed for forty-eight to ninety minutes. This is a very narrow scope, and if this is the primary substantive feedback that teachers are receiving, and if this feedback is the basis for a substantial portion of the teacher's final evaluation, the evaluation may not reflect key considerations that should be included in it. Most importantly, it is missing a clear analysis of whether students are being taught the written curriculum and if students are learning the written curriculum.

As I write this book, many states across the United States are changing legislation to require that teachers and principals are held accountable for student achievement. In the state of Maryland, for example, there is a proposal to increase the weight that student achievement data accounts for on a teacher's evaluation to at least 50 percent of the evaluation. Politically, this proposal looks great. However, in practice, this will be extremely difficult to quantify. What is qualitatively achievable is for principals to ensure that student data is analyzed. More significantly, principals can establish processes to ensure that teachers do not accept poor data without specific plans of action to improve it.

Here are some suggestions to make your postobservation conferences more substantive and accountable for students' achievement:

- Send a letter to your teachers at the beginning of the year discussing your expectations for teaching and learning and the data you will monitor throughout the school year. A sample letter is included in Figure 4.4.

- Specifically, communicate that the following data sources will be reviewed at all postobservation conferences: (2) grade distributions by race, (2) special education and ESOL (English as a Second Language) students' grade distributions, (3) samples of rigorous work and rubrics, (4) unit assessment data, (5) schoolwide formative assessment data.

- In your postobservation written reports, include an analysis of these data sources.

- If the data is not exemplary, determine next steps to support the teacher.

Figure 4.4 Principal's Letter Regarding Observation Expectations

August 2012

Dear Colleagues,

The purpose of this letter is to communicate Utopia High School's expectations for classroom observations for the upcoming school year.

As a leadership team, we decided that it is essential that all teachers receive instructional feedback each school year. We believe that the quality of instruction within our building will be based upon the quality of feedback that is given. Our goal is to affirm all the extraordinary things you do as teachers and to provide support and guidance as needed.

All teachers at Utopia High School will receive one formal observation each semester. Teachers who are in an evaluation year will receive four formal observations: two each semester. In addition, as a leadership team, we have created an informal walkthrough schedule to provide instructional staff with informal feedback throughout the school year. It is also our intent to create subject walk-through schedules for instructional staff to have the opportunity to see the great things that are happening at Utopia High School and to be actively involved in the informal observation process.

We will place an emphasis on the postobservation process during all formal observations. The following are data that we will collectively reflect upon during postobservation conferences:

- Grade distribution data disaggregated by student subgroups
- Unit assessment data
- Samples of rigorous student work
- Samples of teacher-made quizzes and assessments
- Student survey data
- Literacy instruction across disciplines

Together, we will continue to provide our students with a high-quality, world-class education. I look forward to supporting you as we achieve this goal.

Respectfully,

Principal

One very important statement must be made at this point. *As principal, don't play gotcha with classroom data.* Teachers must not be made to feel under attack because their classroom data does not look good. In many instances, you, as the principal, unintentionally created a schedule that placed students with a history of underperformance together in one class to make for a challenging year for a teacher. Your job is not to blame teachers for poor data. Your job is to support teachers in developing plans to improve poor data. Therefore, a teacher's evaluation should not be based solely upon the number of students who are performing well or poorly in class.

It makes sense to evaluate teachers on their efforts, with support, to improve students' data. Teachers' evaluations should take into consideration whether the plan that they employed was research-focused, executed effectively, and revised as needed. A qualitative approach capturing the quantitative results, a research-based plan of action, and the lessons learned will get a school much greater long-term results than a punitive approach that objectively determines success or failure based upon numerical criteria. Poor data and poor processes to improve classroom data should result in poor evaluations.

Distributing Responsibility

As I mentioned earlier in this chapter, as the principal of a school, you cannot be everywhere. However, you have to make your presence known through your expectations. Your job as principal is to make sure that all staff members are doing their job as you expect them to do it. Effective principals understand the power of distributed leadership. In a school where the principal has support from assistant principals and/or teacher leaders who are responsible for providing feedback to teachers, monitoring expectations for feedback is an important process where distributed leadership can be practiced to achieve dramatic results. When I describe distributed leadership, I am referring to the definition offered by James Spillane (2005).

Spillane defines distributed leadership as the interactive web of leaders, followers, situations, and the artifacts and tools essential to the situation. Sorry to get so technical! In layman's terms, and as it relates to the principalship, distributed leadership can be described as a practice of leadership in which the principal interacts with followers (assistant principals and department chairs, for example) in a situation (providing teachers feedback), utilizing tools (observation sheets and protocols) to accomplish a goal. If the quality of the interactions is high, then the overall execution of leadership will be high. Allow me to describe what an example of effective distributed leadership looks like as it relates to the teacher observation process in a school.

The principal and assistant principal of Utopia Elementary School are responsible for completing observations and evaluations of the staff. Both the principal and the assistant principal observe all teachers who are in an evaluation year. The principal has determined that she wants the focus of all observations to be an analysis of student performance through reviewing students' work. The principal meets with the assistant principal to identify who will observe and evaluate each individual teacher. Next, the principal, assistant principal, and members of the instructional leadership team meet to develop a few questions that will be asked during all postobservation conferences. The questions allow for flexibility to ask other questions, of course! During the course of the school year, the assistant principal and the principal complete observations of teachers using the postobservation protocol that was developed. The two discuss how their observations captured their predetermined focus areas, and they discuss the strengths and next steps for each teacher. In this process, both observers are able to review the observation report to determine whether the observer captured evidence of an analysis of student work. When it is time for the teacher to receive an additional observation, the principal and the assistant principal review the previous observation and ask for evidence that the teacher has addressed areas of growth noted then. The two observers look at classroom data to see if results are improving. The principal and assistant principal use each other's observations to complete teachers' final evaluations.

In this example, the situation requiring distributed leadership is the need to complete the observation and evaluation process. The artifact is the postobservation sheet that will be used by both the principal and the assistant principal. The leader could be either the principal or the assistant principal, depending upon who completed the first observation for a teacher. Finally, the interaction occurs when the principal and the assistant principal meet to discuss the data from the observations of each teacher in preparation for the next observation.

By explicitly communicating the need to look at student work and by developing a system to monitor student work, administrators create a "sense of urgency" within teachers to ensure that their students are learning. In addition, teachers are more apt to reflect upon their own teaching and change their teaching practices when the observer is capturing what their data shares and holding them accountable for improving their data.

The Power of a Child's Story

Another powerful way to ensure that student data is at the forefront of your teachers' minds is to utilize the power of a child's story through your data processes. As was stated earlier, it is easy for a school to get totally immersed in data discussions that are focused on percentages and raw numbers of students, and in the process, the school forgets that each number or percentage represents the lives of real children with faces, hopes, and dreams.

Without question, it is important to understand the aggregate data and data by individual student subgroups. This data will enable you to drill down to an individual child's story, and you should use a child's story to awaken the sense of purpose that your teachers will need to understand why you are asking them to continue to work harder, work smarter, and work more effectively. There are two types of stories that can impact the moral conscientiousness of teachers: the success story and the child with promise story.

The Success Story

When people experience tribulations and difficulties, sometimes it is hard for them to see what is working or what is good. You know this from your own experiences. When you are feeling bad, doesn't it seem like everything that happens is bad? I have seen over the course of years that teachers can get overwhelmed in challenging situations when they are trying to get dramatic results in a short amount of time. Without encouragement and support, a culture of despair and a sense that the goals are unattainable can develop.

One major aspect of your job in the first hundred days is to keep people focused and in a spirit of continuous improvement by helping them understand what is good and what is working within the organization. People need to hear from their leader that there is hope that they will be able to accomplish the goals that have been identified by the school, the school system, the state, and/or the federal level. Here is a strategy you can use to accomplish this task:

- Look through your aggregate and disaggregated data to identify the overall improvement areas.

- Concomitantly, look through your aggregate and disaggregated data to identify areas of strength.

- Share both the strengths and areas for improvement with your staff.

- Within the areas for improvement, find a "counterstory."

- Share the counterstory with the staff to set clear expectations of what can happen through their efforts.

So you are probably asking, "What exactly is a counterstory?" I am defining a counterstory as an example of personal achievement that goes against the general perception of performance in that subgroup of student performance at your school. For example, an analysis of your data may reveal that 70 percent of your special education population did not meet proficiency on your most recent reading comprehension assessment. Identifying a counterstory would require you to look at the 30 percent of students who did achieve proficiency and to identify one student whose story can be shared with the staff as an example of what can happen at your school when teachers are determined to improve their special education students' performance in reading. Your job is to create a compelling argument as to why the individual student's performance is not the exception to the rule as it relates to special education reading performance in your school. Counterstories are most powerful when they are shared in person during staff meetings, team meetings, department meetings, or with individual teachers.

The Child with Promise

As we work to ensure all children a high-quality, world-class education, it is important for us to discuss the implications for the lives of our students who do not receive this promise. The reality of education today is that there are "good" children who sit in classes and are not motivated to perform at high levels. Teachers see them every day. Administrators know that these students are in their schools. Yet we do not spotlight this issue. Well, if you want to have a great school, you've got to address it.

So who are these students, and what are their stories? As principal, you have the power of the bully pulpit to ask teachers, "Do you know your students? Do you know their stories?" More importantly, you have the power to highlight individual children's stories as a way of calling your faculty to action. Here are some steps you can take to challenge your staff to look at individual students and their individual stories more closely:

- ♦ Look through your disaggregated data to identify a group of students who are not performing to their academic potential. Alternatively, you may choose to meet with your counselors for them to discuss some of these students with you.

- ♦ Once you have identified some students, take a moment to review their cumulative folders. Note anything of interest, such as attendance data, behavioral data, grade data, special circumstances like divorce or family tragedy if there is information about it.

- ♦ Meet with the students individually to discuss their performance and to ask them their hopes, dreams, and aspirations for the future.

- ♦ Ask students to share what teachers are doing to help them and what can be done to better support them.

- ♦ Use faculty meeting time, department time, team time, or your staff newsletter to communicate anonymous stories about these students to help teachers understand the power that they have to impact children's lives.

Summary

Understanding your school's data is extremely important. You are charged with developing systems, structures, and processes to improve each individual child's life in your school. If you are going to achieve this mission, you must focus your teachers' attention on their individual students' stories, and supports must be in place to make discussions of students' stories a priority in your master schedule.

Reflection Questions and Activities for Prospective Administrative Candidates and Principals

1. How is your school organized to systemically review student work?
2. How has the master schedule been organized to give teachers time to collaborate?
3. What formative and summative data points has your school agreed to monitor?
4. What is your timeline for reviewing key data points as a group and discussing next steps?
5. How does your observation process incorporate student data to create a sense of urgency about underperforming subgroups of students and to celebrate successes?
6. What structure is in place to communicate students' success stories and the stories of students' with promise?
7. Review the definition of distributed leadership. To what degree are leadership actions distributed within your work environment?

Timeline of Activities

July

- Review your school's trend data on key data points for your school district.

- Begin analyzing current data if it is available.

August

- Send staff a letter or memorandum discussing your expectations for observations and the data that will be used to evaluate performance.

- Meet with leadership team to determine (1) what will be monitored, (2) who will monitor it, (3) how data will be monitored, and (4) how students will be retaught and reassessed.

September

- Identify a facilitator for your school's data discussions.

- Meet with your teachers to discuss the nuts and bolts of (1) what will be monitored, (2) who will monitor it, (3) how data will be monitored, and (4) how students will be retaught and reassessed. Allow for teacher input.

- Establish a timeline to review assessments and discuss data at the teacher level.

- Establish a monthly schedule to discuss data with teachers and a facilitator (if possible).

October

- Analyze first-quarter data to identify your successes and your students with promise.

- Meet with groups of students to discuss their performance.

- Share data from student focus groups with staff.

Plan Your Work and Work Your Plan

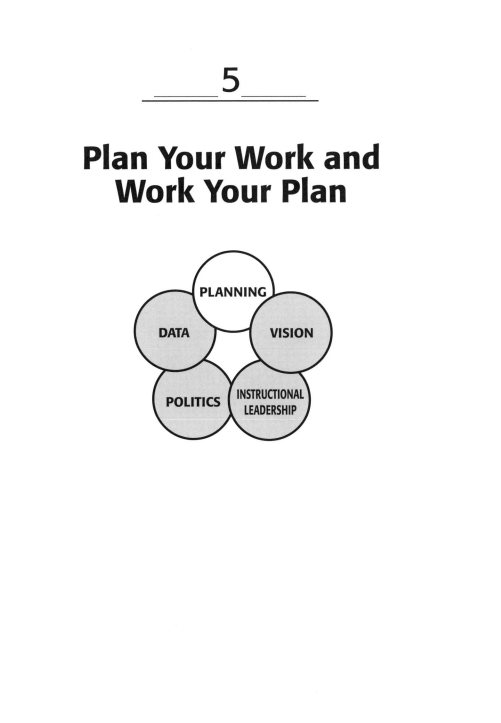

Activities in this chapter support the following principal leadership standards:

Educational Leadership Policy Standards
➢ **ISLLC 2008 Standard 1:** Education leaders promote the success of every student by facilitating the development, articulation, implementation, and stewardship of a vision of learning that is shared and supported by all stakeholders.

National Board Core Propositions for Accomplished Educational Leaders
➢ Accomplished educational leaders drive, facilitate, and monitor the teaching and learning process.

Most school improvement efforts do not fail because a school has not designed a detailed written plan. Now, let's be clear. Some schools do not have written plans that are worth anything. However, most school improvement efforts fail because school teams do not do a good job *executing* the plans. The art of school leadership lies in the school leader's ability to inspire people to execute at high levels to get results for all students. At the core of school improvement efforts is the reality that the effort is only as good as the people who are executing it. This is important for you to remember as you begin to think about the decisive steps you are going to take to build momentum in your school building to improve learning for all students. As you think about the year ahead in your first hundred days, you will need a school improvement paradigm to frame the timeline of your work. Communicating this early will allow your team to understand the cycle of continuous improvement.

An Effective Framework for Continuous Improvement in Schools

In their book *Assembly Required: A Continuous Improvement System*, Lezotte and McKee (2002) make the case for schools utilizing a study/reflect/plan/do framework of continuous improvement. As a leader, you will feel compelled to plan immediate actions and then do "something" to illustrate to the public that your bosses hired someone who knows something! I will urge you to fight the temptation to "plan" and "do" before taking some time to

Figure 5.1 Study/Reflect/Plan/Do Diagram

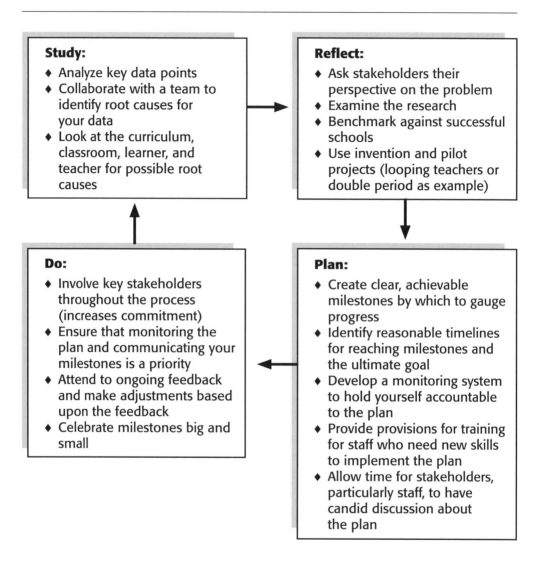

See L. W. Lezotte and K. M. McKee, 2002, *Assembly Required: A Continuous School Improvement System*, pp. 145–193, Okemos, Michigan: Effective Schools Products.

"study" and "reflect." During the first hundred days you will need to take a considerable amount of time understanding the culture that has already been established before you can effect thoughtful change.

One logistical challenge to effectively implementing this paradigm is the timing of your appointment as a principal. Most principals around the country are appointed effective July 1 of the given school year. In most schools, July and August are planning months to prepare for the upcoming school year. New principals are ushered into the natural planning cycle of the school thinking that they do not have time to "study" or "reflect." In many cases, this may be very true! Although the purpose of this book is to advise you on your first hundred days, it is critical for you to understand or have a vision of what should be happening as you look at the entire school year. It is my intent to conceptualize the study/reflect/plan/do framework for you as you look at the entire school year. Although you may be appointed during a time when you are expected to "do" something, you should lead your leadership team through thoughtful discussions about the work that was done to study and reflect upon the school's improvement efforts prior to your arrival.

Figure 5.1 displays a diagram that illustrates the study/reflect/plan/do framework as described by Lezotte and McKee (2002). The remainder of the chapter will delve into the logistics of effectively implementing and executing this paradigm in your school.

Study

During the months of March through May, schools should begin to study their school improvement efforts for the current school year. In most states, this is the time that student testing is occurring, so utilizing staff meetings, department meetings, and/or team-level meetings to evaluate efforts to prepare students is logical. During these months, instructional staff members should explore the answers to the following questions:

- What does our formative data tell us about the effects of our school improvement efforts during the first three quarters of the school year? Are we on target to achieve our stated goals?

- If we do not anticipate achieving our stated goals, did we execute our action plans effectively?

- If we executed our action plans effectively and we still are not anticipating achieving our stated goals, are our action plans addressing appropriate root causes to the problem?

- Have we met with stakeholders (teachers, parents, and students) to discuss possible root causes for not achieving the stated goals?

- What data do we have to tell us whether the interventions we implemented worked for the students enrolled in them?

At this point in the school year, the aim is to predict whether your school anticipates achieving its stated goals based upon the data that you have available. Another aim is to reflect upon your action plans and collectively determine whether they are truly built to address the real problems associated with achieving your goals. Identifying and establishing a clear process to utilize for root cause analysis is necessary during this period.

One fallacy many schools make is that they wait until July and August to begin these discussions. The argument that is made to justify the timing of these activities is that the school will not have its summative data for the current year until the summer, and school staff cannot begin to develop a plan without summative data. I would argue that most good schools know their areas of strength and areas for improvement long before the summative data returns. If a school is closely monitoring formative data, that data should give a clear indication of what the areas of growth will need to be for the following school year. To wait until the summer, when so much work needs to be done to plan, hire staff, and prepare for the next school year, is too late. Another problem is that staff members, parents, and teachers are not easily accessible for input over the summer. School improvement plans that thrive have clear buy-in and input from a broad range of stakeholders. It takes time to have stakeholders truly understand and reflect upon the data.

By the end of May, your school team and community should have a clear understanding of your school's areas of strength and areas of need. Your next task is to reflect upon the best approach to address your areas of improvement.

Reflect

The month of June is an important time in schools. Most schools on a regular school year end at some point in June. It is very easy for teachers to begin to wind down, but this is a time when instruction should still be relevant and important. If your school team spent the last two months studying formative data and critically analyzing plans, time in the month of June should be devoted to communicating proposed school improvement efforts for the upcoming year to staff members and parents. During the months of April and May, your leadership team or your school improvement team spent a great deal of time reviewing data, discussing probable root causes, and discussing action plans. Now, it is important to get meaningful feedback from your entire staff and your parent community as you move into the summer months.

Sustainable improvement occurs only when everyone understands your plan and truly has a say in the plan's development. One reason school improvement efforts often fail is that the implementers of the plan don't really understand why they are doing something or they do not agree with what is being done. The more you communicate with your staff about what you plan on doing and why you plan on doing it, the better plans you will develop. People are very interested in plans that affect their day-to-day work, so it is critical to allow all staff members to engage in the conversation. Consider the following suggestions during the month of June:

◆ Hold small focus groups with all instructional staff members throughout the course of a day during the month of June to discuss your leadership team's analysis of the school improvement process based upon the first three quarters of formative data.

◆ Share what the leadership team has identified as possible causes of the school's results.

◆ Ask staff to share their feedback on what they heard. Are there any factors within the school's control that they think the leadership team should consider? Chart staff members' comments.

◆ Ask staff members what they think logical next steps should be based upon their experiences with their students and the discussion. Chart staff members' comments.

◆ If feasible, facilitate a discussion at a parent-association meeting to gather parents' input.

The feedback that you gain from the parents and staff members will be invaluable for your leadership team to consider as you continue to work over the summer.

In addition to gathering feedback from the staff and parents, once you have an idea about areas of need for your school, you should think about the resources available to research ideas and best practices to support next steps as you develop your plan of action. Consider the following:

◆ What does the research say about the challenges you face? Are there any promising practices that should be followed to guide your work?

◆ Who within your school district is available to support your school and your work? How have you utilized external expertise?

◆ Develop a research action team charged with researching best practices in your challenge areas and identifying resources and supports that can assist your group with thinking about issues.

- Are there schools within your school district with similar challenges and areas of focus with better results? If so, give staff members from your school an opportunity to visit the schools to discuss best practices, review plans, and discuss similarities and differences.

- What out-of-the-district "critical friends" can you utilize to provide an outside perspective on your issues?

These are important considerations as you move into your summer work. Too often, schools become islands of isolation and, in the process, fail to critically reflect upon what research has identified as best practices or gain support from both internal and external support systems. Identifying these support systems and sources of knowledge will ensure that your summer work is both productive and meaningful.

Plan

July and August are busy months in your first hundred days. As was mentioned earlier, most appointments are effective July 1, so, technically, you will walk into your new job not knowing what has been done prior to your arrival. At this point, getting feedback from your staff and conducting a root cause analysis to base your school improvement goals upon may be difficult.

One recommendation is for you to reflect upon the questions that were identified for the "study" and "reflect" sections of this chapter. Although you may not be able to perform these activities, you can get an idea whether these activities were conducted by your predecessor, and there may be some data available for you to review prior to officially meeting with your leadership team.

When your leadership team meets in July, this is the time that you want to look closely at all your summative data points. You should be able to evaluate whether your school has achieved the school improvement goals that were set in the previous year. If feedback is available for your team to review from staff, parents, or students, you should read this data and look for trends.

During the planning stage, you and your team will develop your student achievement goals for the school year, as well as the action plans that will communicate how you are going to achieve your goals. This is a very difficult task to accomplish during your first year as a principal because so much about your work environment will be new to you. You may understand how to develop a school improvement plan that fulfills the requirements that your school system has communicated to schools, and you may know how to create clear "stretch" goals that will compel your school to work hard to achieve. However, you may not know the instructional staff you are working with or their level of commitment and ability to effectively execute the plan that you design. Thus, your first year's plan may be the weakest of your tenure. As you move into year two and you are able to begin the study/reflect/plan/do cycle from the beginning, you will be in a much stronger position to develop a stronger plan.

As explained in an earlier chapter, your job during this planning season is to really listen to your staff members and try to understand their habits. Observing people as they interact to develop the school's comprehensive plan will give you lots of valuable information. Specifically, as you observe the process, you should note the following:

- Who are the formal and informal leaders?

- Who seems to have the strongest understanding of the status of your school?

- Who keeps the discussions focused on the needs of the students?

- How inclusive has school improvement planning been at your school? Who has historically been invited to develop your school improvement plan?

- What evidence do you have to suggest that the previous year's plan was closely monitored?

- How well do the leadership team members interact with one another?

- Do you see issues with trust, accountability, a fear of conflict, an inattention to results, or a lack of commitment to the work?

Regarding the actual development of the school improvement plan and the components of an effective school improvement plan, I would suggest that you review the following books, which are easy reads, to give you a substantive foundation for the development of your action plans and goals: *Assembly Required: A Continuous Improvement System* by Lawrence Lezotte and Kathleen McKee (2002); *Data Wise* by Kathryn Boudett, Elizabeth City, and Richard Murnane (2005); and *Data Analysis* by Victoria Bernhardt (2004).

Once your plan has been developed, one of the most important components of your plan is your system for monitoring it. Your plan should be monitored frequently and you should provide a substantial amount of time (at least one hour) for your team to review action items from your action plan,

Figure 5.2 School Improvement Plan Monitoring System

Goal to be monitored	Person(s) responsible for monitoring and reporting	Date of report	Date of report	Date of report	Date of report	Date of report	Date of report	Date of report	Date of report
Goal #1 Action Step 1									
Goal #1 Action Step 2									
Goal #1 Action Step 3									
Goal #1 Action Step 4									
Goal #1 Action Step 5									
Goal #2 Action Step 1									
Goal #2 Action Step 2									
Goal #2 Action Step 3									
Goal #2 Action Step 4									
Goal #2 Action Step 5									
Goal #3 Action Step 1									
Goal #3 Action Step 2									
Goal #3 Action Step 3									
Goal #3 Action Step 4									
Goal #3 Action Step 5									

Figure 5.3 Process for Monitoring the School Improvement Plan Monthly

♦ As a leadership team, identify one date per month that the team will monitor goals and action steps in your school improvement plan.

♦ On a chart, identify the goal and action step that will be monitored and determine how often that particular goal should be monitored throughout the school year.

♦ On the chart, place an X on the dates a goal and action step will be monitored.

♦ Identify the person who will be responsible for leading the efforts to monitor the goal. This person will also collect data and report to the leadership team on the progress of the goal.

♦ Use a consistent shell to provide a written report updating progress on goals.

♦ As a team, decide on next steps.

♦ The leader responsible for monitoring the goal will follow up on next steps with the appropriate team working to improve the goal.

evidence of the goal being completed, evidence of results to show that the action is having an effect or not, and next steps. Some aspect of your school improvement plan should be monitored monthly at a minimum. Figure 5.2 shows a sample spread sheet that can be used to monitor your school improvement plan frequently. Figure 5.3 describes a process for reporting on your school improvement efforts with your leadership team. Figure 5.4 (page 112) is an example of a reporting shell for the leader to give to leadership team members. This shell can also be shared with your community to keep everyone updated on your school improvement progress.

In addition, be sure to discuss the staff training that will be needed to effectively execute your plan. You will need to rely on your leadership team to openly discuss the strengths and weaknesses of teams as you look at the actions in your school improvement plan. You cannot make the assumption that people will know how to do what you have written in your plan. Again, school improvement plans do not achieve their goals because of a lack of will. Most often, it is a lack of skill that holds teams back. As a result, you will need to build in the professional development that is needed for your team to effectively execute.

Figure 5.4 School Improvement Plan Reporting Shell

Reporter(s) name(s):

1. What is the goal that is connected with this update?

2. Share an update on activities related to this task.

3. What specific data have you monitored to demonstrate progress toward this goal?

4. Does the data show that the school is making progress toward this goal? Explain.

5. Identify next steps.

6. Group input.

Ultimately, you were hired to improve results for all students. That is the long-term goal. In your first hundred days, you want to look for those opportunities to show people you have listened to concerns, and there are no concerns that are too small. At this point in the summer, you should be thinking about your quick wins. As you review the results of the previous year's school improvement efforts, ask yourself the following questions: What were the main concerns from the previous year? Are there any concerns that are easy to address? Is there something that is glaringly broken that you can focus on as a starting point?

Consider the following common quick win areas:

♦ Is your building clean? Does it need to be painted? Are the exterior aesthetics appealing (e.g., gardening, landscaping, signage, and trash receptor locations)?

♦ Order new banners communicating your school's vision or core values. Display them outside the building and at the main entrance.

♦ Create posters of students and staff and display them in picture frames throughout the building.

♦ Ensure that the bathrooms are clean of graffiti and operational.

♦ Ensure that a team has reviewed your discipline policy.

♦ Send a welcome letter to parents.

- Randomly call individual families from each grade level to acquaint yourself with your new community.

- Take a bus tour of your community with your faculty.

When your staff members return to begin the school year, it will be essential for you to review the goals of your school improvement plan. Ideally, you should be able to give them the feedback that they gave you prior to their leaving if it was collected, and you can share how their feedback and suggestions have been incorporated into your plan. If your school did not have the opportunity to solicit their feedback prior to your arrival, it is essential that you provide your staff an opportunity to review the goals that have been created and the action plans that have been developed. As the ultimate executors of the plan, their feedback and support are essential for effective implementation.

Do

Once your plans have been vetted by your staff, it's execution time! Your plan should be visibly displayed for your staff and community to see. Posting your plan on your school's Web site or making a copy of your plan available in the main office or media center will let your community know that you are proud of the work you plan on doing during the course of the school year.

Each month, as you evaluate your school improvement efforts, send an e-mail to your community through a list-serve or in your school's monthly newsletter regarding the updates on your school's progress. Ideally, you should have parent participation in your school improvement planning meetings. If not, it is a good idea to invite parents to attend. When parents have clear information about what your school is doing to support all children, they will be more likely to support the school as needs arise.

As you are evaluating school improvement efforts, it is important for you to celebrate milestones along the way. Examples of things to celebrate include effective implementation of plans, incremental improvements, student participation or staff perceptions of programs, as well as volunteer efforts and external supports. Staff and students need to be constantly made aware of your appreciation for their commitment and hard work. If you wait until the end of the year to determine whether you have something to celebrate, you will miss opportunities to maintain momentum along the way. As the principal, you are the school's number one cheerleader, and staff, parents, and students will be looking to you for encouragement!

Summary

The study/reflect/plan/do model of continuous improvement is a simple, yet effective way to frame your thinking about the school improvement process. You must give detailed attention to effectively executing school improvement initiatives. In your first hundred days, you will want to reflect on what has happened prior to your arrival, and you will need to forecast what is to ultimately come as you lead your school into the future. Your encouragement, know-how, and enthusiasm will get you off to a great start.

Reflection Questions and Activities for Principals and Prospective Administrative Candidates

1. Does your school effectively implement a study/reflect/plan/do framework for school improvement efforts?
2. What are potential barriers to implementing a study/reflect/plan/do framework in your school or school district, and what can be done to overcome these barriers?

Timeline of Activities

July

♦ Assess the work that was done between May and June as it relates to school improvement planning.

♦ Assess how school improvement planning has been historically conducted.

♦ Review the previous year's plan.

♦ Begin drafting your current plan.

August

♦ Continue working on school improvement plan.

♦ Determine how frequently your goals will be monitored, who will be responsible for the goals, and the evidence you expect to analyze as you monitor your goals.

September

♦ Review the school improvement plan with staff members and receive their feedback.

♦ Make adjustments to the plan.

♦ Identify staff training needs.

♦ Place your plan on the school Web site.

October

♦ Begin monthly progress updates of your school improvement plan.

♦ Celebrate milestones, however big or small.

Master Timeline for the First 100 Days

July

- ◆ Update the school Web site with a welcome letter and picture.
- ◆ Create a picture show to share with your constituency.
- ◆ Meet with immediate supervisor and/or board members.
- ◆ Schedule meet-and-greets with staff and parents throughout the community.
- ◆ Begin creating a graphic of your beliefs and vision of teaching.
- ◆ Collect belief statement surveys from the community and staff.
- ◆ Read leadership team personnel files and most recent evaluations.
- ◆ Meet individually with leadership team members.
- ◆ Review the evaluation criteria used for leadership development team members.
- ◆ Update the school Web site.
- ◆ Write a welcome letter to parents and staff.
- ◆ Complete a graphic display of beliefs.
- ◆ Schedule meet-and-greets with parents and the community.
- ◆ Schedule a designated time to meet with your secretary daily.
- ◆ Review your school's trend data on key data points for your school district.
- ◆ Begin analyzing current data if it is available.
- ◆ Assess the work that was done between May and June as it relates to school improvement planning.
- ◆ Assess how school improvement planning has been historically conducted.
- ◆ Review the previous year's plan.
- ◆ Begin drafting your current plan.

August

- ◆ Collect belief statements from parents and staff.
- ◆ Identify public relations team and begin brainstorming activities that will be highlighted.

- Collect belief statement surveys from the community and staff.
- Read teacher observations done by qualified observers in your school from the previous year.
- Assess how your leadership team members used their time prior to your arrival.
- Identify a book for your leadership team to study with you.
- Identify celebration activities and processes.
- Begin to identify culture brokers and begin scheduling meetings.
- Place feedback cards in the main office and on the school Web site.
- Set after-school activities on your calendar.
- Schedule monthly achievement events for students.
- Send staff a letter or memorandum discussing your expectations for observations and the data that will be used to evaluate performance.
- Meet with leadership team to determine (1) what will be monitored, (2) who will monitor it, (3) how data will be monitored, and (4) how students will be retaught and reassessed.
- Continue working on the school improvement plan.
- Determine how frequently your goals will be monitored, who will be responsible for the goals, and the evidence you expect to analyze as you monitor your goals.

September

- Create a year-long calendar of events and meet with local media.
- Develop and share a "pride points" PowerPoint display to share at Back-to-School Night and post it on the school Web site.
- Begin weekly automated calls to parents if available.
- Begin sending list-serve information, Twitter information, Facebook information, and monthly Web site updates.
- Collect belief statement surveys from students, community, and staff.
- Share schoolwide data at Back-to-School Night and at different forums to educate the community about the educational status of the school.
- Create the school's teacher classroom observation schedule.

- Communicate your leadership priorities to your leadership team in writing.
- Develop your leadership team's meeting schedule for the year, including individual check-in meetings with your leaders.
- Begin writing staff commendations.
- Begin weekly staff letters, bulletins, and e-mails.
- Begin monthly web messages, blogs, and Twitter messages.
- Begin meetings with student groups.
- Solicit feedback at Back-to-School Night.
- Visit malls, places of worship, supermarkets, and gathering places with the public relations committee.
- Identify a facilitator for your school's data discussions.
- Meet with your teachers to discuss the nuts and bolts of (1) what will be monitored, (2) who will monitor it, (3) how data will be monitored, and (4) how students will be retaught and reassessed. Allow for teacher input.
- Establish a timeline to review assessments and discuss data at the teacher level.
- Establish a monthly schedule to discuss data with teachers and a facilitator (if possible).
- Review the school improvement plan with staff and receive their feedback.
- Make adjustments to the plan.
- Identify staff training needs.
- Place your plan on the school Web site.

October

- Begin analyzing belief statements if you have a sufficient number from each constituency group.
- Begin discussing packaging of the belief statements and developing a draft vision statement to be shared and revised with the community over the next two months.
- Send honor-roll information to the local newspaper and post it throughout the building.
- Give leadership team members feedback on their work.
- Continue identifying and meeting culture brokers.

- ♦ Continue visiting malls, places of worship, supermarkets, and gathering places with the public relations committee.
- ♦ Analyze first-quarter data to identify your successes and your students with promise.
- ♦ Meet with groups of students to discuss their performance.
- ♦ Share data from student focus groups with the staff.
- ♦ Begin monthly progress updates of your school improvement plan.
- ♦ Celebrate milestones, however big or small.

Resources

Arbinger Institute. (2002). *Leadership and self-deception: Getting out of the box*. San Francisco, CA: Berret-Koehler.

> This is by far one of my favorite books on leadership. In a very simple parable, the book discusses self-deception: the act of not knowing or resisting the fact that you may have a problem. The book challenges you to think about your interactions with other people and your reactions to other people. The concepts in this book are so powerful that I have shared it with staffs and I frequently revisit it.

Bolman, L. G., & Deal, T. E. (1995). *Leading with soul: An uncommon journey of spirit*. San Francisco, CA: Jossey-Bass.

> This will have your school leaders reflecting upon the importance of understanding their own leadership journey and having a sense of "self" as a leader. Leadership is about more than completing tasks and fulfilling deadlines. It's about personal fulfillment and releasing potential, and this book will bring these thoughts to the forefront in your school.

Collins, J. (2001). *Good to great: Why some companies make the leap . . . and others don't*. New York , NY: William Collins.

> This is probably one of the best management books written over the last decade or so! This book focuses on excellence by researching companies that have moved from good to great. Recently, Jim Collins published a monograph that focuses on good to great in the social sector—another must-read for principals and school administrators.

Constantino, S. M. (2008). *101 ways to create real family engagement*. Galax, VA: Engage Press.

> This book is an excellent resource that discusses 101 practical ways to increase engagement between families and schools. The examples can be immediately implemented within your school.

Covey, S. R. (2004). *The 7 habits of highly effective people*. New York, NY: Free Press.

> This will give your staff an approach to attain their goals as they seek to improve personally and professionally. Covey's principles will

allow your staff members to critically evaluate their own performance and determine which areas of their professional growth need to be developed.

Epstein, J. L., Sanders, M. G., Simon, B. S., Salinas, K. C., Jansorn, N. R., & Van Voorhis, F. L. (2002). *School, family, and community partnerships: Your handbook for action.* Thousand Oaks, CA: Corwin Press.

> This book provides empirical research on parental involvement based upon a research-oriented framework that was developed by Joyce Epstein. This book is powerful because it clearly identifies research that supports the need, importance, and effects of parent involvement in schools.

Gladwell, M. (2007). *Blink: The power of thinking without thinking.* New York, NY: Backbay Books.

> This really forces leaders to think about how to make effective decisions. What I love about the book is that it challenges readers to understand themselves and think about what is most important in making a decision. The goal is not delving into tons of data, but rather thinking about what is most relevant and being confident in making the decisions you make once you understand and trust your gut!

Gladwell, M. (2002). *The tipping point: How little things can make a big difference.* New York, NY: Little, Brown.

> This is a book about change. Gladwell discusses the conditions in which change occurs through very engaging stories. This book made me think about the types of people that are needed if change is going to occur in schools.

Linsky, M., & Heifetz, R. A. (2002). *Leadership on the line: Staying alive through the dangers of leading.* Cambridge, MA: Harvard Business School.

> This takes a critical look at the practice of leadership. Leading schools in a way that promotes excellence and equity for all children is dangerous work, and these authors will provide your staff with a theoretical framework from which to look at their work. In addition, it offers practical advice on how to survive as you navigate the perilous waters of public education.

Johnson, S. (1998). *Who moved my cheese?: An amazing way to deal with change in your work and in your life*. New York, NY: Putnam Adult Press.

> This is another classic about the change process. This parable is a great read for staff to discuss the cycle of change and the feelings most associated with the change process.

Lencioni, P. (2002). *The five dysfunctions of a team: A leadership fable*. San Francisco, CA: Jossey-Bass.

> This looks at the pitfalls teams may hit as they try to improve an organization. This is actually one of the best books I have ever read on teamwork. The author identifies five dysfunctions teams face, and his points will help you analyze your school team to diagnose and correct poor team performance.

Maxwell, J. C. (2001). *The 17 indisputable laws of teamwork: Embrace them and empower your team*. New York, NY: Thomas Nelson.

> This is another great book about teamwork. Maxwell shares seventeen aspects of teamwork that will guide a team's thinking about leadership and the importance of working together.

Maxwell, J. C. (2007). *The 21 irrefutable laws of leadership workbook: Follow them and people will follow you*. New York, NY: Thomas Nelson.

> This focuses on leadership. For new leaders in schools, Maxwell's twenty-one principles are easy to understand and apply to your current situation.

Phillips, D. T. (1993). *Lincoln on leadership: Executive strategies for tough times*. New York, NY: Warner Books.

> This is a great Leadership 101 book that details the leadership strategies of one of our country's greatest presidents. Phillips, through a critical lens, captures many facets of Lincoln's leadership style that would be very appropriate and effective for leading a school!

Schmoker, M. J. (1999). *Results: The key to continuous school improvement* (2nd ed.). Alexandria, VA: Association for Supervision & Curriculum Development.

> This explores how school leaders can effectively monitor data to improve student results. This is a very practical book that school leadership teams can read together to begin to critically reflect on the importance of data and how to monitor it effectively.

References

Bernhardt, V. L. (2004). *Data analysis for continuous improvement* (2nd ed.). Larchmont, NY: Eye On Education.

Boudett, K. P., City, E. A., & Murnane, R. J. (2005). *Data wise: A step-by-step guide to using assessment results to improve teaching and learning.* Cambridge, MA: Harvard Press.

Cooke, W. J. (1995). *Strategic planning for America's schools.* Arlington, VA: American Association of School Administrators.

Council of Chief State School Officers. (2008). *Educational Leadership Policy Standards: ISLLC 2008.* Retrieved January 1, 2011, from http://www.ccsso.org/Documents/2008/Educational_Leadership_Policy_Standards_2008.pdf

Gabarro, J. J. (1987). *The dynamics of taking charge.* Boston: Harvard Business School Press.

Gladwell, M. (2002). *The tipping point: How little things can make a big difference.* New York, NY: Black Bay Books.

Henderson, A. T., Johnson, V., Mapp, K. L., & Davies, D. (2007). *Beyond the bake sale: The essential guide to family/school partnerships.* New York, NY: New Press.

Hill, L. A. (2003). *Becoming a manager: How new managers master the challenges of leadership* (2nd ed.). Boston, MA: Harvard Business School Press.

Joseph, S. (2010). School district "grow your own principal" preparation programs: Effective elements and implications for graduate schools of education. *International Journal of Educational Leadership Preparation, 2*(1), 1–14.

Leithwood, K., Louis, K. S., Anderson, S., & Wahlstrom, K. (2004). How leadership influences student learning. Retrieved from http://www.wallacefoundation.org/KnowledgeCenter/Knowledge Topics/EducationLeadership/HowLeadershipInfluencesStudent Learning.htm

Lezotte, L. W., & McKee, K. M. (2002). *Assembly required: A continuous school improvement system.* Okemos, MI: Effective Schools Products.

Maxwell, J. C. (2005). *Developing the leader within you.* New York, NY: Thomas Nelson.

National Board for Professional Teaching Standards. *National Board Core Propositions for Accomplished Educational Leaders.* Retrieved January 1, 2011, from http://www.nbpts.org/products_and_services/national_board_certifica?print=on

Saphier, J., Haley-Speca, M. A., & Gower, R. (2008). *The skillful teacher: Building your teaching skills* (6th ed.). Acton, MA: Research for Better Teaching.

Spillane, J. P. (2005). *Distributed leadership. The Educational Forum 69*(2), 143–150.

Watkins, M. (2003). *The first 90 days: Critical success strategies for new leaders at all levels.* Boston, MA: Harvard Business School Press.